PRAISE FOR THE BOOK

"Twelve years ago, I wished I had this book to help me navigate through my first CISO job. Back then, the "CISO" title is still an evolving role and there were not many of them. This book is not just a collection of stories nor a CISO primer – this is a treasure-trove for any cybersecurity professionals who are looking for that CISO blueprint. There is no single path to this role and there are numerous ways you can fail or succeed in this job. In this book, you will see the different paths taken by the authors, the challenges and obstacles they encountered and the different strategies they used to be successful at their jobs. This practical CISO leadership book will help aspiring cybersecurity professionals navigate their career as well as any experienced CISO to understand and apply the insights and pathways conveyed in this book."

CeciltheCISO is a Sr Director of Consulting Practice at Critical Start and former CISO at DFW Int'l Airport

"One of the biggest challenges in cybersecurity today is that we don't share our stories. The problem with this approach is that the next generation of cybersecurity professionals will have to learn all the same lessons from scratch. The CISO Mentor is the answer to this, sharing powerful insights from some of the best leaders in the cybersecurity field today. For anyone wanting to become a CISO this book is a must read "

George Finney, J.D., CISM, CISSP
Chief Security Officer
Southern Methodist University

"I am a fan of books that are written by practicing and experienced CISOs like CISO Mentor. I was not surprised to see that some of the authors are members of the CISO Executive Network. I am confident other CISOs, especially new and rising security leaders, will find it valuable to read CISO Mentor and glean the knowledge the authors have to offer. A recommended reading for any aspiring CISO."

Bill Sieglein, Founder, CISO Executive Network

"The personal journeys so well written in *CISO Mentor* bring to life the many paths to the complex CISO Role, as well as demonstrating the benefit of diverse backgrounds and experiences to achieve cybersecurity leadership success.

Todd Fitzgerald, author of best-selling *CISO COMPASS: Navigating Cybersecurity Leadership Challenges with Insights from Pioneers*

The CISO Mentor

Pragmatic advice for emerging risk management leaders

from experienced, award-winning practitioners

Zartech, Inc.

Dallas, Texas

Zartech, Inc.
2203 Longview Rd
Irving, TX 75063, USA

www.zartech.net
email: info@zartech.net
phone: (214) 631-9353

Book edited by Paola Saibene and cover designed by Abu Sadeq.

Ordering Information:

Quantity sales. Special discounts are available on quantity purchases by corporations, associations, and others. For details, contact the publisher at the address above.

Printed in the United States of America

ISBN: 9798588658737

First Edition

100% of all profit from this book will be donated to charities.

About the publisher of this book

Zartech is a U.S.-based corporation where their mission is to empower organizations to obtain greater cybersecurity maturity. Zartech helps organizations improve their cyber security defenses, reduce business risk, and meet regulatory compliance needs. Their team of senior level security practitioners has worked at both small and large companies and government organizations around the world.

Zartech offers a unique IT GRC solution called Cyberator® that helps more effectively identify/manage cyber risk by leveraging its intelligence in merging and mapping cybersecurity frameworks against the organization's existing and future posture, providing automatic tracking of all identified gap remediation efforts, along with full control of security road-map development. It provides the essential elements of a GRC platform but is also a great solution to manage other areas of an information security program such as vulnerability management, policy management, security incidents, and vendor risk. Cyberator® also helps organizations become compliant with the data privacy laws of 80+ countries.

For additional info, please visit: zartech.net

The team at Zartech is honored to help publish this great collection of literary work from highly prestigious practitioners in the field of information security and risk management.

Contents

LEADERSHIP JOURNEY

By Ian Schneller

When I examine my career, which has spanned nearly three decades in many job roles to include two positions as Chief Information Security Officer (CISO), leadership is at the foremost when I think about my successes and challenges along the way. Numerous books and courses are dedicated to the topic, and so I won't focus on a textbook approach to leadership. Rather, I will share my perspective of leadership and provide you methods and 'thought drills' you can use to assess where you are along your journey and what to expect at the next stage.

I entered the United States military at a young age and eventually retired after several decades. That fine organization understands that leadership is critical to the current and long-term success of the organization and to the country. For that reason, formal leadership training is not only a topic taught during initial training programs, it's a career-long commitment. The profession not only includes official leadership training at several points in a career, it also reinforces continuous development with a defined career path of enhancing skills in positions of more and more influence and importance.

Your Journey

What does this mean for you? The study and application of leadership is a career-long endeavor. If your goal is to be a CISO, then you should make a commitment to study and continuously evolve your leadership skills. Rarely will a CISO be chosen based on technical prowess, but many times, company leadership will choose a CISO based on their ability to lead teams to achieve organizational objectives. While every person's history will differ, a common path for you will likely start out as an individual contributor and then moving up the ranks from small team leadership to organizational leadership. In each step, you'll have more responsibility with more impact to your decisions, and at the same time, you'll have less day-to-day interactions with the person or persons you report to. This means your success becomes less of what you do and more of what those in your charge accomplish. As your career progresses, you'll find that you'll need to be much more of a generalist in topics rather than a deep technical expert in any particular subject. Each journey will be different for each person, so think of this chapter as a model that you should tailor to your strengths and goals.

	Career Stage	Impact	Expertise	Influence	Interactions w/ Manager
Individual Contributor	Entry	Tactical	Technical	Mostly within current team	Frequent (Several times daily)
Small Team Leadership	Early	Mostly tactical with opportunities to develop strategic planning	Still rely a great deal on technical but starting to become a generalist	Information Security Organization	Occasional (2-3 times per week)
Large Team Leadership CISO	Mid to Late	Strategic	Generalist	Company-wide and even perhaps industry	Less Frequent (Once per week)

Table 1: Summary of Characteristics in your Leadership Journey

Individual Contributor

When you start your career, perhaps right out of college or after graduating from any number of high quality training programs, you'll likely start as an individual contributor. Don't think this doesn't mean your ability to develop as a leader is limited. This is a wonderful opportunity to develop a key skill of leadership – Followership. Being an effective follower is a pre-requisite in your leadership journey. In fact, you will not become an effective leader without developing this critical skill. At this phase, focus on becoming an expert in your assigned duties, while consistently, with high quality results, meeting your supervisor's objectives. As you do so, your goal is to become the one sought-out for advice by others. As I watch teams to determine who future leaders will be, I watch to whom different professionals go when seeking assistance, especially if those individuals are outside of the current team.

> *A note about technical expertise... Being a technical expert is different than being a technology expert. The route to CISO may or may not depend on being a strong technologist, but it does depend on becoming a technical expert in some area. In this context I use "technical" as being an expert in your profession. Your area of expertise may be in firewalls, regulations, compliance, or threat intelligence. All are areas one can become a technical expert, but not all require expertise in technology. This is an important distinction to make.*

Practical Application: Consider that you are an information security compliance analyst who tracks compliance according to Securities and Exchange Commission (SEC) regulations. One indicator that you are on the right track is if your legal department seeks your opinion about the impact of a new draft SEC regulation. As well, you receive high performance markings for being complete and accurate in assigned roles.

Small Team Leadership

Congratulations! You've proven to be someone with excellent followership skills and are an expert in at least one technical area. Your supervisor has recognized your potential and has selected you to lead a small team. You may be called a team "manager," but don't fall into a common trap of confusing leadership with management. There are many writings on the difference, and I highly recommend you read them, but suffice to say for now, you will need to learn the difference and ensure you develop BOTH managerial and leadership skills. This period is often a very difficult transition because now you are personally accountable for what your team achieves, not just what you achieve. Recognize this position of increased authority for what it is – a test. Your leadership team knows that this can be a tough transition, and while they are there to help, they also want to see how you motivate and take care of your team. This may be your first-time supervising someone, and so your leadership transition must focus on learning how to take care of those under your charge. Are they trained? Have you set objectives for them? Are you available when they need you? Are they staying with your team or looking for jobs elsewhere? How is their morale? One indicator your supervisor will want to see, in addition to high performance, is observing how many people want to be on your team while at the same time determining if there's an exodus of talent out of your team. In this position you still need to rely on your technical expertise and will likely have many interactions with your supervisor.

Practical Application: Building upon our last example, you are now the manager of a team of compliance analysts who ensure compliance with multiple regulations. Your supervisor knows you were an expert in SEC regulations and so will want to see that you're developing the "new you" and not doing the work you left behind. Rather, your supervisor wants to see that all team tasks are on track, in this case, that the work aligned to NIST Cybersecurity Framework is on track too.

Large Team Leadership

Wow! You've performed superbly as a small team leader, and now you've been asked to lead a large team. In this case, you likely have a team of teams, all with their own leader. Your focus will now change, and your leadership skills now must shift to becoming less of a deep technical expert and more of a generalist. You will perform fewer direct technical actions, and will be setting objectives for your teams. What should the team be doing? Why does the objective matter? How do we know when we've achieved the objective? Are the teams well resourced in terms of people, budget, and authority? At this stage in your career you'll likely report to the CISO, and she will be relying on you to help her lead the entire organization. In doing so, you'll likely spend a bit less time with your direct reports than your prior job, and more with your peers, both within the information security organization as well as elsewhere in the organization at large.

> *A note about "WHY?" - One challenge you'll face is building leaders and teams that will make the right decision. The real world is very complex, making it nearly impossible to have a clear decision matrix for all events. By continuously explaining "WHY" behind each decision, you'll train your leaders to make appropriate decisions. I personally recommend "Start with Why" by Simon Sinek as a great book that all students of leadership should read.*

Practical Application: You now lead the entire Governance, Risk, and Compliance organization reporting to the CISO. You got here by being a compliance expert, and along the way, you likely learned key concepts of governance and risk too. Now, although you rely on your direct reports to be experts, you also have a seat at the CISOs table with your peers. In this position, you will be expected to set larger strategic objectives for the information security team that cross into security operations and identify/access management. You will do well, because your professional education along this journey has exposed you to many different components of an information security program. You've also built a wide network of professionals within the information security organization and industry, and that is now serving you well. Now, if not already, you will need to understand how the organization works as a whole and develop relationships with leaders in those areas.

CISO

You've made it! After years of hard work, you've made it to your goal of being a CISO. Your focus now will certainly be less technical and much more strategic in nature. Another large change you'll immediately notice is that you are now part of the top leadership cadre in the company. As such, you'll be expected to participate in strategic planning on nearly all facets of the business. By now, you should be very familiar with your company's financial information, risks, growth strategies, market opportunities, and weaknesses. While you'll still be graded according to information security 'scorecards,' you'll also be more and more held accountable to being graded according to the financial growth of the organization; in other words, you're a key stakeholder in the direction of the company. Your focus will be to ensure you have a strong leadership team implementing short- and medium-term information security objectives so you can focus on larger issues. A key component to this is ensuring they are well resourced with headcount and initiative funds to ensure your organization is well protected against an agile and ever-evolving cyber threat adversary. No longer will the month- or year-long horizon be your limit. You should now be focused on multi-year strategies and ensuring continued organizational support, culturally and financially.

Practical Application: The Board of your manufacturing firm is interested in increasing revenue by ensuring customers have in-house options to finance their large purchases. The decision has been made to purchase a financial services firm to implement just such an option. As CISO, you'll need to strategically plan for the impact to your current team. What are the differences in regulation with a financial services firm? How should the information security team be aligned in your current organization, post-acquisition? What capabilities do you now have that can take the place of the acquired team's capabilities? How mature is the new team? All of these questions force key strategic decisions that you'll need to make, and then convince the Board to agree to, in order to make the acquisition successful. As an example, since you've become a trusted leader in the firm over the years, you successfully argue that you need additional resources focused on financial systems compliance, as well as a deputy CISO whose job is to act as the CISO of the newly acquired firm.

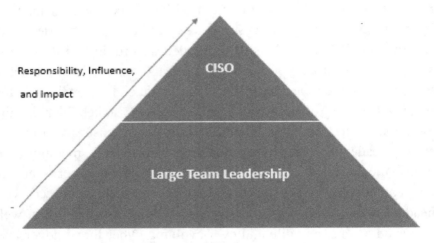

Figure 1: Leadership Journey Model

Helpful Lessons

Many books on leadership are available that expand in depth on many principles barely touched upon in this chapter. In the small space left, I would like to share a few practical lessons to help you on your journey. As you do, you'll find your sphere of influence continuously expands, propelling you towards your goals.

1. Be a student of leadership – continuously! Read, read, and then read some more. I personally enjoy reading biographies of

leaders, focusing on how they approached and solved issues, rallying a large team along the way. If you're lucky enough to be in an organization that sponsors leadership development education, sign up for each and every opportunity.

2. Know your stakeholders, both members of your team, peers, and leaders. By understanding their strengths, weaknesses (we all have them!), and goals, both personal and professional, you'll be able to both lead and follow them. This requires you to invest in their development, which means you need to set aside time to spend with them. Don't be that leader that is too busy to see their direct reports.

3. Be Persistent! Expect failures – they will happen. When failures happen, reflect on why and do better next time. This will require a great deal of personal integrity as you self-reflect as well as when you discuss the circumstances with your team and leadership.

4. Accept the Challenge! Many times, as a leader, I've asked someone to tackle a tough problem. I don't just need someone to help me (Spoiler Alert: I don't know the answer either!), I also want to discover who my leaders are. I know that no one knows exactly how to tackle the challenge I laid out, but I do know we can achieve it together. I am looking for those leaders who can say, "I don't know how to do this now, but I'll figure it out." Most of my career successes have started out as, "I have no idea how to do this." As you tackle that challenge, you'll grow as a leader, eventually building a very strong brand of someone who can lead through challenging times.

5. Communicate! Those under your charge as well as those you report to want to know what's on your mind. Explain your goals and

reasons ("The Why") for actions. As you do so, you'll build a team that is able to become more and more effective in achieving organizational objectives because everyone is aligned to a common cause.

6.   Challenge Respectfully. As a leader, the times that I'm most worried are when no one challenges plans. I know that plans are rarely correct, especially the first time written. I value and reward those that will respectfully challenge and then work to create an even better plan.

7.   "Yes, if..." Don't be the person that says "No" all the time. Think in terms of "Yes, if..." Yes, we can finish the firewall installation this week, IF we rearrange priorities so that the budget presentation is drafted next week instead. See the subtle difference? I find this attitude helps immensely by allowing all to know you're on the same team while also providing the trade-offs. Try saying "Yes, if..." the next time you want to say no. You'll find it quickly changes how you influence others.

As you embark on your journey, I expect that you'll see additional paths that I didn't mention here. The journey to CISO is a complicated one, and there is no one set formula. This is but just one. I encourage you to find mentors who can guide you on this journey. However, I do expect completely that if you embrace the principles in this chapter, that you will be successful!

About the Author

Ian Schneller is currently the Chief Information Security Officer (CISO) of a publicly traded US firm. His past roles have included key information security leadership positions in large US banks and the US Government. During his multi-decade service in the military, Ian served in multiple executive roles to include as CISO, Commander, and cyber advisor to US Congress. Ian has authored or contributed to multiple publications, and is an oft invited speaker to events including RSA and the FS-ISAC. Outside of work, Ian enjoys spending time with his family, preferably anything outdoors.

LinkedIn Profile

Chapter 1.2

QUESTIONS AND ANSWERS THAT WILL IMPACT YOUR CAREER

By Sonja Hammond

We have all heard our parents and the generations before us say, "If only I knew then, what I know now!" As a child, teen, or young adult, these words cause eye rolling and conjures hopes that the phone will ring, or something will happen to get you out of listening to the adult wisdom that is sure to follow. It is true that many prefer to learn things in their own way, and on their own time. However, when you are trying to pursue a desired career path, suddenly you are open to hearing wisdom from those who have been down that career path already. With this in mind, I share these thoughts around answering some questions that arise when you pursue a career path that may lead to being a CISO.

Do I need to know IT?

My CISO career path began after I had spent 15 years in Information Technology (IT). While in my first information security role, universities started offering courses in cybersecurity. Not long after, cybersecurity degree programs became a part of most college catalogs. I was envious of the idea that a person could get a bachelor's degree in cybersecurity and enter the workforce as a cybersecurity analyst with little to no previous experience. It seemed like the ideal plan if your goals were to work in information security or cyber security and someday become a CISO. Recently, I started to understand that there is more to the CISO career path than having a cybersecurity degree. This is where the questions began.

It is common for college graduates to ask, "Should I get a master's degree?" I find that cybersecurity students ask themselves, "Should I build my technical skillset?" The short answer to this question is "yes." However, it is how you acquire that technical skillset that has huge implications and significant impact on the trajectory of your career path to CISO. If your plan is to study and pursue some technical certifications, that may not result in the desired impact of getting to CISO more quickly. Certifications are important and frequently help you land that next role, but if you do not demonstrate your technical knowledge in the workplace, you will not progress as quickly towards a management position and eventual CISO title. The real answer to the question of building your skillset is this: study for the CISSP, build a computer, build a network, get to know active directory, learn some networking skills, and take every opportunity that you get to sit in IT working sessions to understand technical challenges and how they are addressed. You need to understand the basics of technology and the tools used in IT. As CISO, you will someday be discussing the use of a load balancer to build resilience into your security tools one moment and discussing network access control to slow the possible spread of malware the next. Your understanding does not have to be as deep as a practitioner's is, but you do need to understand enough to discuss such topics and provide guidance. On top of this, you also need that CISSP certification.

What is more important – technical expertise or team fit?

As you travel the path towards a CISO role, management skills become a defining factor in your ability to lead. A question that comes up during this part of your career is, "Do I hire for technical expertise or team fit?" Every person that I talk to immediately answers this question with, "both!" It is true that the ideal information security or cybersecurity candidate will have strong technical skills, great communication, and be a positive team fit. Seldom do all those things come together in one individual. Over many years of hiring, here is what I have learned. You have to find a person that can do the job, which makes technical expertise important, but if you hire someone that is not a good fit with the existing team (assuming you intend to keep the existing team members), it is team fit that can bolster your capabilities and put you on a faster leadership track. This is not to say that you hire someone with little to no technical expertise, but it does mean that you may not hire the most skilled technical professional, if that individual has poor communication skills and will irritate or aggravate others. Personality and communication style will affect every person that the individual interacts with, not only within the team, but also outside of the team (e.g., customers). As a leader, you look for team cohesion, but you do not want someone who will upset the customer, which is essentially everyone.

Knowing the importance of team fit should help when interviewing. You will want to look for a good mix of technical expertise, communication skills, and positive team fit. As previously stated, this can be a real challenge. I frequently find one candidate with exceptional technical expertise and another with impressive people skills demonstrated by good communication and positive team interactions. Rarely do I find someone with all of these qualities. As a result, I look for and hire someone with the potential to learn additional technical skills. I have found that it is easier to build a person's skillset than it is to change their personality.

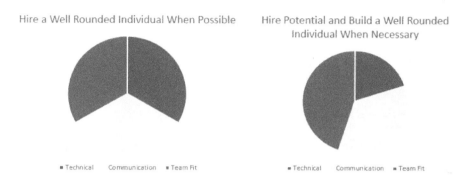

Hire a Well Rounded Individual When Possible

Hire Potential and Build a Well Rounded Individual When Necessary

■ Technical   Communication   ■ Team Fit   ■ Technical   Communication   ■ Team Fit

So, here is a successful hiring strategy: first, define a baseline of the minimum skillset that you can accept for the person to fill your open roll; second, build a training plan for the individual that will help raise them to the desired level of technical knowledge; third, define the soft skills that will bring success for the person that fills the open role. Lastly, determine if you should supplement the new employee with a seasoned consultant until the new hire completes some of the required training and begins to apply the newly acquired knowledge in their day-to-day job.

One final thought specific to hiring is that even with the best hiring plan, sometimes a person's potential or lack of potential is not apparent until they have been in the role for some time. You must remember that part of being a leader is also being a coach and you will have to provide direction and course correction when appropriate. Invest in each new hire as if he or she will become your strongest team member. Should the individual fail to grasp the necessary technical expertise, or turn into an ogre, you will be able to terminate them knowing that you did everything in your power to give them the opportunity to become well rounded and capable of meeting the needs of the role.

How do you say yes?

As you climb the leadership ladder, your ability to say yes becomes a critical skill. Anyone in a security role knows we have been labeled as the group that says no to everything. To reach the CISO role, you must realize that the executive team wants to hear two things:

Yes, we can do that, and we can do it securely.

In short, no one wants to be told no and if you are labeled as the person who says no frequently, it will be difficult to attain that CISO title. This is where honing your sales pitch comes into play. First, you want to give people hope as this builds a positive relationship. When they ask to do something that has security implications, you need to have a response that avoids saying no, you need to have plans for further discussion, and you should commit that you will work together to find a final solution. Even when you are certain that what the person is asking to do cannot be done securely, you must refrain from saying no, and still work hard to find an alternative method to achieve a similar outcome.

What are the budget must-haves?

Information security and cybersecurity bring a unique set of requirements when it comes to tools. As the threat landscape changes, compliance requirements expand, privacy brings new scope, and technology is developed to address new threats, the tools in your toolbox must change. Tools are a significant portion of any technical leaders' budget, but there are other items that will enhance your ability to flex and maneuver when something unexpected comes up. In addition to tools, you will need to budget for employee compensation; but what other items do you need? In general, every budget needs a contingency plan. For instance, you may need a budget for some consulting to help with implementations or staff shortages. Make sure you allow for training, certifications, and possible travel for people on the team. Do not forget that most tools are moving to cloud and SaaS offerings that cannot be capitalized, thus you will need operating expense dollars for new tools. Finally, be sure to include a couple of nice-to-have items that you can live without should budget cuts come your way.

Are you a good fit for a role in security?

I was once told by a person that had been working in cybersecurity for about five years that he wanted to make a career change. I admit this was the first time anyone had said this to me, so I felt compelled to understand what was pushing this individual from a career path that offers growth and challenge every single day. Initially, this gentleman stated that he did not want a role that came with the possibility of being called after hours or on weekends due to a data breach or malware attack. I questioned this response, because the environment was mature and calls outside of business hours were rare. I also knew that he was looking at an IT role that would include being on-call at least one week out of every month. The reasoning did not make sense.

Over the coming weeks, I continued to watch and listen in hopes of finding the real reason this talented individual wanted to make a career change. After a morning conversation over coffee, the cause became clear. It wasn't really about the on-call nature of working in security–it was about mental stress. As I listened to this gentleman talk about what he was looking forward to in his future IT role, I found some common characteristics of working in a cybersecurity environment that was causing him constant mental stress. The first was that security is a thankless job, meaning there is very little (if any) recognition for the work that is done. It is much like changing the batteries in smoke detectors. It is extremely important that the task gets done and in a timely fashion, but never will you receive a thank you for doing it. Security is seen as necessary just like any type of routine maintenance, except there is very little that is routine about it. This lack of routine is what leads to the next mental stress trigger.

Information security and cybersecurity have some routine tasks where people habitually check alerts and respond to incidents. However, I frequently find that each day turns out different from what was originally planned and very little of my day is routine. Security teams must be nimble and able to adapt to the needs of the business. They also have to be adaptable for times when malware finds a weakness and gets into the network. Even if your security program is mature, there are constant triggers that shape the day of each security professional. Triggers can come from project teams that have started down a path without considering data security, or from a business development team that is closing a deal, but didn't consider how they will securely exchange legal documents with an outside law firm. Other triggers may be targeted cyber attacks or the release of a zero-day patch that must be tested and pushed out immediately. While planning is necessary, seldom will a day go quietly and as planned. For some individuals who are primarily task driven, prefer well defined project work, or who need significant structure to their day, security is not going to be a good fit and mental stress will be a constant issue.

After many conversations with the gentleman who decided to change careers, I found a third mental stress trigger that is specific to information security. This was a stressful matter that I had never considered before. The man described his discomfort in being exposed to sensitive information. In security, we frequently work on topics that are confidential and not common knowledge publicly or within the company. Sometimes these topics are so sensitive that anyone working on a specific project may be required to sign a stringent confidentiality statement. As a long-time security professional, I see this as a normal operating procedure, but for others, this is a major mental stress trigger. It is not just the act of signing paperwork that creates stress, but the fact that the individual knows something so sensitive that they have to make sure they never mention or comment on the matter outside of a defined group of people. For many, this creates mental stress. They spend time thinking about what would happen if they accidentally said something about the top-secret project to someone who was not aware of it. As a result of thinking about accidentally disclosing sensitive information, the person becomes nervous around others and anxious in meetings. Sometimes you can even see their discomfort and you may notice changes in their behavior. One example that I noted once I became aware of this mental stress trigger was that individuals who struggle with the responsibility of knowing confidential information will go from being outgoing and excited to attend a team lunch to a reclusive introvert that eats lunch alone. While they may seem like a far-fetched example, I witnessed this exact behavior following a person having to sign a project confidentiality statement.

It was the three mental stress triggers described above that pushed the gentleman, who performed his cybersecurity role very well, to change his career path. Recognizing that some people are not as adaptable as others is now a topic that I explore when interviewing candidates for a security role.

What is one powerful thing that I can do to support my team?

As a leader, it is important to realize that even the best and most professional people will show signs of stress when outside their comfort zone. In cybersecurity, it is during ransomware attacks or malware infections that your team will look to you for strength, confidence, guidance, leadership, and most of all, a demonstration of how to handle stress. I am not saying that you must be completely calm and collected during these incidents; but you should work on how to present yourself during stressful scenarios. Just as you take your team through tabletop exercises to prepare them for incident response, you should also practice how you will respond and perform during these situations. You may not get it perfectly, but just walking through a situation before you experience it allows the brain to train for the performance. It is like practicing for a public speaking event, or a performance in a play; so, do yourself and your team a big favor and practice for your performance of leading during stress. It is a confident and less emotional response, during a highly stressful event that will empower your team and give them the support they need.

About the Author

 Sonja Hammond is the Vice President, Chief Information Security Officer for National Veterinary Associates and is a Chair Member of the Governing Body for the Evanta Dallas CISO Community. Sonja is an author and public speaker with over 30 years of IT and Cybersecurity experience. She has developed information and data security programs for several global organizations including Callaway Golf, Hewlett-Packard, and Essilor.

LinkedIn Profile

Chapter 1.3

THE STEP-BY-STEP GUIDE
By Abu Sadeq

As I reminisce on my past career and decide on what to write about in this chapter, I am amazed that it has been 26 years since I started my professional career as an analyst for a small healthcare company in Dallas, Texas. Over time, I ended up working in different industries, but the most exciting time of my career was when I joined a global organization as their head of IT, with the responsibility of information security. Information security was not my forte at that time. This chapter covers some of the challenges that I faced, how I overcame them, and the lessons I learned.

Since the advent of the internet, businesses of all sorts, sizes, and locations have tried to explore new and larger markets to capture. It has provided them with new opportunities for which they work competently, efficiently, and effectively with computerized tools. In this day and age, every acknowledgeable business that uses the internet must create a cultural security strategy to gain consumer trust, goodwill, and confidence. In such a susceptible business environment, cyber security should be an active part of any business plan to ensure its safety.

The first question I had to ask myself was "how secure is our organization?" To answer this question, I needed to first understand the 'lay of the land' by doing a comprehensive assessment of its operating environment and its specific business needs. As part of the assessment, we looked at what we have, where it is, how it is currently being secured, what kind of safeguards we have in-place, whether we have continuous monitoring and detection processes, or if we have proper response planning and disaster recovery capabilities in place. In addition, sensitive data needs to be located and classified along with assets including hardware, software, IoT devices, and cloud resources. I view information security as a risk mitigation activity and a holistic assessment of threats and vulnerabilities that help an organization appropriately prioritize and mitigate its risks. The assessment that we conducted gave me a very good idea of the strengths and weaknesses of the security program and the security culture of the organization.

I also needed to understand how our industry and business operated. Without knowing this, I would not have been able to envision the problems that we might encounter and how to solve them. I ended up spending some time on the company's manufacturing floor and in the service centers. This helped me understand our operations and obtain the needed business acumen for this task. I strongly feel that the IT/Security leader must be a technical expert with the business acumen to have successful conversations with boards and executive teams. This is one area that I had to improve over time, as my background has been mainly in the technical side. We can lose our executive audience and confuse them if we are using too many business jargons in our speech. If our top management does not understand us, they will be hesitant to act on our recommendations. Boards and executives care about business; and cyber risks can threaten the two major goals of any business, which are profits and highly important business operations. Cybersecurity is an important business function, so it needs to be presented to the top management like all other important business functions in the company.

As a next step, a very clear conversation had to occur with the organization's senior management and/or the Board regarding the acceptable level of risk for the data and information that needs to be protected. It is important to identify who has risk authority for assuming and signing off on cyber risk. The Board and the CEO should ultimately hold delegation authority for risk decisions. The CISO or CIO should also be able to make security risk decisions in the same way that a CFO has the authority to make financial risk decisions that are enterprise-wide. Business unit leaders should have a degree or security risk authority for some risk decisions that are largely contained within their business units. I highly recommend identifying potential risk-decision scenarios and performing hypothetical discussions on what would happen.

An already defined tolerance for risk is important for your organization. The National Institute of Standards and Technology's (NIST) Special Publication 800-39[1] defines risk tolerance as *"the level of risk or degree of uncertainty that is acceptable to organizations and is a key element of the organizational risk frame."* Risk tolerance is the risk above the appetite that might be acceptable for an organization. While it may seem like setting cyber-risk appetite may be just technical, there is more to it than that. There are conversations that need to include non-technical functions. Cyber-risk appetite ties different types of risks including cyber risk, enterprise risk, and operational risk.

Businesses are driven by different factors. Some are driven by customer security requirements while others are delivered by compliance. Then there are also those organizations that are driven by their IT system's security risks.

An organization's security pressure posture is also vital in determining the risk tolerance level. Security pressure posture is something that represents the external drivers and forces that compel businesses to implement a strong security program. Organizations with a moderate to high security pressure posture will have several factors driving their need for a strong information security program. They are usually attractive to cyber attackers for financial reasons (e.g., valuable data or other ways to make money from a compromise) while also feeling various levels of pressure to have a strong security program from customers, the business, and/or regulators.

There is no generally accepted security risk assumption model template. We went with the risk tolerance levels of low, medium, and high that can be applied to an organization and after having a workshop with the leadership team, we came up with our risk tolerance level that helped with the development of our security strategy and determining funding/resource needs. A formal process for security risk assumption that is both documented and approved by the top management is an important first step in developing a security strategy. The goal is to develop and implement a security program that is not only effective, but also sustainable.

Low	Medium	High
•Organizations with multiple compliance requirements or sensitive data have extremely unacceptable level of risk tolerance. Does not accept risks that could result in a significant impact of its operation.	•Organization with a 'medium' risk tolerance level, may have some sensitive data and/or compliance requirement. Depending on business impact, will need strong security controls for their activities.	•Usually, organizations have a high cyber risk tolerance level if they don't have any sensitive data or any compliance requirements. As a result, they don't have a need to implement and maintain strong security controls.

Ref: Risk tolerance level descriptions

To ensure alignment with the business, I had to work with other department leaders within the organization and my own team to ensure that the security program's goals were tied back to the overall IT and business-level goals. Through these cascading series of business, IT, and security goals, it became easier to explain how a security initiative can help businesses achieve their goals. I highly recommend having multiple sessions where open discussions on planned business and IT initiatives are held.

Building out the security strategy and roadmap

The cybersecurity industry has fed and, to a large extent, continues to feed off fearmongering. As a result, organizations are spending millions of dollars on shiny security products that are not needed to block most hacks! The current strategy of most organizations layering on different technologies is not only proving ineffective, but it is also overly complex and expensive. An ideal option for the security of businesses would be to adapt a risk-based approach that carries out a holistic assessment and analysis of business threats, in its current and future operating environment, and then mitigate those threats.

The information security and risk management strategy will provide the business with direction for protection of information infrastructure that ensures the capabilities provided are in alignment with the business goals and the organization's risk profile. Structured methodologies can be great for businesses. These methodologies can help you get authentic insight by assessing IT security implications and understanding business objectives.

I did not see any reason to re-invent the wheel and decided to leverage a well-established security framework to build out the security roadmap. Ultimately, the implementation of a cost-effective cybersecurity framework included careful considerations on how we identified, protected, and recovered critical assets, as well as how we detected and responded to security breaches. While we cannot avoid all cyber risk - we need to identify, mitigate, and reduce it to an acceptable level. Fortunately, there were several good frameworks such as the ones from the National Institute of Standards and Technology (NIST),[1] International Organization for Standardization (ISO),[2] and COBIT 5.[3] I decided to adapt the NIST Cybersecurity Framework or CSF,[4] which has a high adaption rate.

The Framework for Improving Critical Infrastructure Cybersecurity (CSF or NIST Cybersecurity Framework) is a tool originally developed for the private sector that agencies must implement to manage cybersecurity risk. The CSF can serve as the foundation for a new cybersecurity program or a mechanism for improving an existing program.

Businesses can use CSF for identifying cybersecurity risks, assessing cybersecurity risks, and then continuously managing cybersecurity risk. It can help an organization determine which activities are most important to critical service delivery, prioritize expenditures, and maximize the impact of investment. The CSF is designed in such a way that it can support existing business practices and cybersecurity operations. It allows you to express your cybersecurity requirements to your customers and business partners. It can also help in identifying gaps in your business's cybersecurity practices. The CSF also lays out the processes for considering civil liberties and privacy implication in the cybersecurity program.

The Framework is made up of three components as follows: the Framework Core, Profiles, and Tiers. Organizations can use these three components together to conduct a comprehensive review of their cybersecurity program. The main component of the Framework is the Framework Core (the Core). The Core presents a variety of cybersecurity related activities that can be found in a cybersecurity program, such as the performance of vulnerability scans and the detection of malicious code. The activities are classified into five main groups or functions— these functions are:

1. Identify
2. Protect
3. Detect
4. Respond
5. Recover

Each function is divided into categories and subcategories of cybersecurity outcomes and activities.

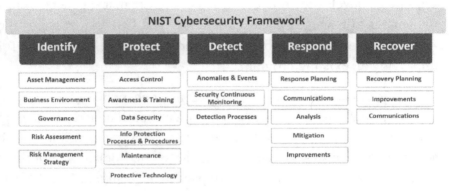

Ref: National Institute of Standards and Technology (NIST)

If a security roadmap is implemented effectively, it can be very helpful in mitigating risk. It can also help in defining actions when a compromise is detected. A clear road map will ensure that you mitigate risks while keeping a strong focus on your business goals.

With our assessment completed, gaps were analyzed against a defined control framework. Certain steps were defined to measure and fill these gaps. I would like to emphasize here that it is important to map the cybersecurity framework against the existing and future posture of the organization. Based on our organization's risk acceptance, goals, and objectives, a visual representation of the suggested initiatives was developed and detailed within a 1 to 3 years roadmap. This roadmap included all sorts of relevant information including investment summary for investment in processes, technology, and people that can align our skills and capabilities with the control framework of the business. Activities were sequenced so that they can provide a more effective implementation plan, where the projects were prioritized based on risk.

To help prioritize the initiatives on our security roadmap to ensure business objectives are realized, or security gaps addressed, we drew upon our mission drivers, a cost/benefit analysis, and understanding of risk to achieve the outcomes in our objectives. Next, we determined the resources necessary to address the gaps. For each identified activity or control that needed to be in place, we identified whether the organization met or did not meet the best practice in developing our cybersecurity and risk mitigation plan. For any risk that we decided to not "mitigate" and "accept," we documented the risk posed by not implementing the best practice, putting compensating control in-place, and obtaining the sign-off from the risk owner.

Build Top-Down

We proceeded as follows: The goal was to build a strong security program that was well designed, implemented, and managed. The security program is made from many layers and it will operate best if a top-down approach is followed. Therefore, we started by defining the 'Vision' – a descriptive picture of the desired future state – "Where do we want to be?" Next, we needed to identify the 'Objectives' – the High-level achievements of the security program. We wrote down the 'Goals' – anything that was measured to help fulfill an objective. Next, we documented the 'Strategy' for each of the goals

29

– those actions we implement on a day-to-day basis to achieve our objectives. (There could be one or many 'Projects' associated with each 'Strategy' – These are concrete actions an organization takes to execute its strategic plan.) The last step in building the security program was to identify the 'Capabilities' that need to be in place to create business value, i.e., log monitoring, remote access, access management, incident management, etc.

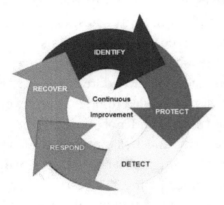

Building the security roadmap is not a one-and-done project; it should be part of a continuous program strategy and operations cycle. You can never entirely mitigate cyber risk. It is not something that can be achieved as an end result; instead, it is a continuous process. You need to take certain steps in order to mitigate cyber risks. As you take each step, the business becomes more and more secure and stronger against cyber risks.

The cyber risks keep evolving and your business may face new risks with passing time. To cope with the changing risks, you need to implement processes that ensure continuous mitigation of cyber risk. Beyond the technical processes and procedures, as security professionals, we should also be familiar with the latest legislation and regulations that organizations have to abide by and adjust to our roadmap as necessary.

Tracking and Communicating Goals

It does not matter how well the information security leader understands the business goals and build out the security roadmap, it is all for nothing if that information is not communicated to the security team. In order for the security projects and programs to be effective, the concerned people should know the end goals they are trying to achieve. On the other hand, top-level employees should also know about the opportunities and risks associated with the actions and inactions of the security team. The communication strategy must include both the security team and senior leadership, and in some cases all employees. The flow of communication needs to be in both directions: top-down and bottom-up communication must be in concert with one another.

Information security is very important in the 21st century. The key performance indicators should link with employee performance and key imperatives of the business. This will show that information technology is taken seriously in your business. Making information technology KPIs part of your business strategy will also be great for the Information Security Management System (ISMS). There can be different types of Information Security (IS) KPIs ranging from policy metrics, business related metrics, and technical metrics. These key performance indicators are very important for reaching your business goals and objectives.

About the Author

 Abu Sadeq is currently the Founder and CEO at Zartech where his mission is to empower organizations to obtain greater cybersecurity maturity. Abu is a certified Chief Information Security Officer (C|CISO) and has a Master of Science degree in Management Information Systems from the University of Texas at Dallas. He has diverse industry experience in Aerospace & Defense, Chemical, Telecom, Healthcare, Oil & Gas, and Consumer Goods. Abu has extensive experience in creating strategies and plans that define IT/Security operational excellence. Abu is also the creator of *Cyberator®* an innovative cybersecurity, governance, risk, and compliance solution.

Abu Sadeq is an honoree on the 2021 ***Forbes Next 1000*** list of US entrepreneurs who are redefining business amid unprecedented uncertainty.

LinkedIn Profile

References

1. *NIST SP 800-39:* The purpose of Special Publication 800-39 is to provide guidance for an integrated, organization-wide program for managing information security risk to organizational operations (i.e., mission, functions, image, and reputation), organizational assets, individuals, other organizations, and the Nation resulting from the operation and use of federal information systems. Special Publication 800-39 provides a structured, yet flexible approach for managing information security risk that is intentionally broad-based, with the specific details of assessing, responding to, and monitoring risk on an ongoing basis provided by other supporting NIST security standards and guidelines.

2. The *National Institute of Standards and Technology (NIST)* was founded in 1901. NIST is a physical sciences laboratory and a non-regulatory agency of the United States Department of Commerce. Its mission is to promote innovation and industrial competitiveness. NISTs activities are organized into laboratory programs that include nanoscale science and technology, engineering, information technology, neutron research, material measurement, and physical measurement.

3. The *International Organization for Standardization (ISO)* is an independent, non-governmental organization, the members of which are the standards organizations of the 165 member countries. It is the world's largest developer of voluntary international standards and it facilitates world trade by providing common standards among nations. More than twenty thousand standards have been set, covering everything from manufactured products and technology to food safety, agriculture, and healthcare.

4. *COBIT 5*: COBIT (Control Objectives for Information and Related Technologies) is a framework created by ISACA for information technology (IT) management and IT governance. The framework specifies a set of generic processes for the management of IT, with each process defined together with process inputs and outputs, key process-activities, process objectives, performance measures, and an elementary maturity model.

5. *NIST Cybersecurity Framework (CSF)*: Set forth by the National Institute of Standards and Technology under the United States Commerce Department, the Cybersecurity Framework is a set of guidelines for private sector companies to follow to be better prepared in identifying, detecting, and responding to cyber-attacks. It also includes guidelines on how to prevent and recover from an attack. Version 1.0 of this framework was published by the NIST in 2014. A recent security framework adoption study reported that a majority of the surveyed organizations see NISTs framework as a popular best practice for computer security, but many note that it requires significant investment.

Chapter 1.4

NOT FOR THE FAINT OF HEART

By Chuck McGann

Why do you want to become a Chief Information Security Officer?

This is a great question that everyone aspiring to the top position in security should consider. Is it for the money, the prestige, the possible career path expectation? Once you answer this question honestly, you can plan the journey accordingly. The CISOs job does not start at 8 a.m. and end at 5 p.m.–it is 24/7; the threats keep on coming, and people make mistakes - this job is NOT for the faint of heart. This job takes commitment at the highest level. You will have holidays, birthdays, anniversaries, and vacations impacted. You will get calls in the middle of the night to deal with things and ask yourself in the morning, "Did that really happen; did I really answer the phone?"

As a CISO, you must set the bar for honesty, integrity, and compliance. Your function is that of the "watcher" looking to find bad things being done and bringing those things forward to protect the organization, regardless of who is involved – friend or neighbor, superior, peer, or subordinate. You will impact people's lives through your policies and compliance enforcement in your duty and quest to protect the organization. This is the job of a CISO, and you need to answer honestly why you want this position, because it will offer no mercy.

Where Do You Start?

Now that you know why you want the CISO position (being honest) you have to understand the skillsets needed and where you fall short or excel in these skills. In my opinion, a college degree is a requirement, not a "nice to have." I also advise CISO "wanna be's" that an advanced degree – MBA, MS in Information Security, or the like, are pretty much the "price of admission" to the selection pool for the CISO position.

A solid technical background is almost a requirement (or should be) for reaching this role. The rationale is for a CISO to have an understanding of the infrastructure, the technologies, the integrated environment, and the business value of the services provided. A CISO must also understand the business model of the organization and the competitive environment in which they are engaged. I've asked many security professionals on the CISO career path and only 60% of those queried could cite to me their organization's mission statement (I did not ask for a verbatim recitation). This is a critical measure of a CISOs engagement with the business. If you don't know your organization's mission, how can you develop and manage a security program and define a risk management strategy.

CISOs should be well versed in the business applications supporting the mission of the organization and spend time with those business owners to build a solid trusted advisor relationship. They should build a common understanding of the value of those applications, and how a poor protection and recovery strategy can put the organization and those that depend on it– customers, partners, and stakeholders–at serious risk.

Finding Mentors

Mentors can be peers, senior leaders, or subordinates. These resources may not always be from your own discipline and are often from business units supported by your organization. Electing a mentor or mentors is a cooperative effort. The mentor and mentee must agree on the value of the relationship and what the expectation of the relationship is. It's important to determine the needs of the mentee and ensure that the mentors can provide a level of "expertise" in those areas. You should not look for a mentor guiding you in technical acumen if the mentor is not experienced in that area.

Mentors come from all walks of life. You, as the mentee, should do an honest objective skills assessment to understand areas of need. It is also important for the mentee to do a deep introspective evaluation as to what growth areas exist, from where you can learn, and how to do better. What are your perceived (from others and yourself) shortcomings, and who can best help you address these needs for a positive outcome?

Your dependence on your own honest assessment of needs and your reliance on objective feedback from peers, family, and friends, are critical to obtaining mentors in the areas of need. You can have more than one mentor. I've had several mentors at one time, mostly when encountering new challenges such as job promotions, new assignment, or employment changes.

Employment change is the area where a mentor can make the difference between a seamless integration into an organization or a time full of challenges and misunderstandings. Understanding the culture and organizational politics can play a large role with your acceptance of your new role. Your hierarchical position on the corporate structure can be impacted by missteps, and this is where a mentor can truly be your savior. A mentor can provide the backstory on "who's who," who and what group has the most influence and why, and what person or persons might be a challenge for you. Finding the right mentor or mentors is not easy and admitting to yourself at the CISO level that you don't have all the tools to do the job is difficult, but leave your ego out of the equation, select someone that knows the organization and the ropes, and you will be on your way to success.

The Challenges

The challenges for a CISO are many and the support structure can often seem to evaporate in the face of adversity. These peer networks can be achieved with membership in various certification agency local and national chapters and connections on various social network and chat platforms.

As a CISO, you are expected (rightly so) to understand the technology in use, the infrastructure upon which it functions, the business systems dependent on both, and the threat landscape for the present and foreseeable future. You will hear the previously unrecognized threats – read "zero-day exploits" are no excuse to be unprepared for the impact that might result. You should have planned for that, even though the vendor did not, still… you should. A challenge? Yes, indeed! How do you absorb those types of situations where possible derogatory comments come your way, and they question your ability? You prepare yourself for these types of issues with a solid strategy and 'defense in depth' tactical protection suite of tools.

The CISO does not have, in most cases (otherwise it might violate the separation of duties rule), any ability to actually implement any technology changes – other than what is under their own control, perhaps security tools (event collectors, the SEIM, Pentest/assessment tools) and analytic-type applications.

The technology is managed by the IT organization and they are responsible for upgrades, implementing the CISO required protections, and keeping the software up to date. Herein often lies the conflict. In the world of "uptime" performance measurements, maintenance windows are dedicated to application upgrades and corrections. Trying to drive a security tool update/upgrade into this limited time slice is often impossible, and if the infrastructure is not architected properly, then it is truly impossible.

Security upgrades must be tested, as should all system upgrades – that's a given. However, there may be times when a security upgrade is required to prevent a critical outage or prevent a threat from impacting the organization. These "interruptions" often require the highest levels of approval and they should, if a negative business impact is possible or customer experience is at stake.

Understanding the culture of security in your organization is paramount to understanding how security needs will be viewed – beneficial or maligned, you have little control of that perception if you are new to the position. If you have been the CISO for a period of time and you have not been able to influence the culture to accept security as a viable business imperative, you need to review your strategy, work with your mentor(s), and determine a different and more effective course of action. Often, this can start with the Information Technology leadership. Discuss with IT the symbiotic relationship you have and how you are dependent on each other for ensuring the organization is successful. These conversations are not easy and sometimes they are ego bruising, but they must occur and can have significant influence in the perception arena for the stakeholders.

Security, like the network, will be the bane of all others' operational problems and existence. If the network didn't cause the poor performance, then there must be a security change that rendered the application unusable or drove it to a degraded state. There will be times where this will be the case – a critical update, a filter set error, a misconfiguration, or a vendor change that does not map to the technology currently running. There may be other times when the IT upgrades have outpaced the security upgrades, also causing an issue.

When this happens, stand tall and admit the impact, address the issues and why this occurred, and what the plan is for corrective actions to return to a normal state, and then share what the prevention plan is for the future. This is not done in a vacuum; it is done with the stakeholders AND the technology support teams – everyone needs to understand the issues and commit to making the processes better.

CISOs must maintain their honesty and integrity to remain effective in the position. If you don't have an answer, don't make one up – investigate and provide one within a reasonable period of time. As CISOs, we are charged with maintaining the Golden Triangle of Confidentiality, Integrity, and Availability. We do this working through the organization's stakeholders. The expectation/challenge is that we must be right all the time, but the reality is that you need to be smart enough to know when you are not right, and engage the people that are smarter than you to get it right.

Mentors and mentee's both benefit from the relationship if treated properly, the Mentor educates, and often rediscovers something they had forgotten and the mentee learns through others' experiences and develops a trusted advisor relationship helpful in providing guidance in difficult or uncertain times.

Acquiring the Skills:

So where does a CISO acquire all these skills to be the know-all, be-all, and soothsayer of the threats that are yet to manifest themselves? It starts with understanding your organization, and what's important to the success of the company. A CISO should have experience in different areas of the organization. Many CISOs work their way up from an IT position or a privacy function and move through either the Security Operations Center or the Business Impact Assessment side of the security organization. That's not to say that other functional experience is a limiting factor, it's not!

Understanding technology is critical and understanding the current technology architecture in use and the network infrastructure is a must. So, back to the mentor discussion. If you are weak in these areas, look for a mentor that can help you learn and understand the environment. If you came over from the IT side, how much do you know about the business and how the business functions? What applications are critical to success and which ones bring customer satisfaction? How is money made and on what cycle does it flow – is the organization seasonal or cyclical, is it level funded, sales dependent, or budget allocated from a central source (government)? What makes this organization work? If you don't have this knowledge, then you are again back to the mentor discussion and you need to find a well-established source that can educate and inform you as to the current processes and influencers driving the organization to mission success.

Certifications are a fantastic way to show the acquisition of a skillset, but they are not a replacement for experience, knowledge, and talent or aptitude. Some people do not test well and thus may never attempt a certification exam; others can ace them without much trouble. A certification is not the be-all and end-all, nor is it a college degree. They are additional tools in the toolbox; they are experiences that you can rely on for additional support when you are confronted with a difficult situation. Experience is often the best teacher and this is where you will understand what to do and what not to do – often the "what not to do" is more important to understand. In either case, be prepared to have the skills to make some decision.

CISOs should have an advanced degree, but at a minimum, an undergraduate degree. I'm not trying to be "elitist" here, and I did say that a college degree is not a limiting factor, but I will tell you that within the peer space of your organization, without a degree, you might experience a feeling of isolation, that your opinions have less value than those that have the paper hanging on the wall. Through your degree studies, you will acquire skills in relationship building, compromise, leadership, and adaptation that will serve you well in the corporate ranks. You are not at the top and you should never think you have all the answers.

The best skill you can acquire is to surround yourself with people that enhance the security function and bring the best knowledge and capabilities they can to drive the organization forward with success; and to know when you are failing – self-awareness can be a difficult skill to acquire but it is the one you will need the most.

Learning the Politics

We are not talking about political parties here – Democrat, Independent, or Republican, or whatever your country uses to delineate one group from another for purposes of governing. We are talking about office politics, which can be far more devastating for the CISO and their function.

My first IT Manager's position with a very large quasi-government agency brought me a lesson I'll never forget, and I share this with those I mentor and teach. I'd been the IT Manager (position was new to the organization and me) for about four months. A peer, the Finance Manager, called me in to her office for a chat. She asked how I was doing and what did I think of my move, and of the organization. I was pretty honest and said that I thought I was coming to an organization that was better than where I was before, more technically advanced and with highly skilled resources, and I found that this was not the case.

She smiled and agreed with the assessment and then provided some details on how the current situation had evolved, how staff had been assigned, and funding allocated. Overall, she intimated that the creation of the IT department had taken resources and authority away from other functions and there were undertones of hostility to what had occurred – "turf" issues were at play. We discussed objectively what that meant and why, and that she was opposed to the overall creation in the beginning. Nevertheless, as responsibility was off-loaded to the IT department, her group was able to focus on other issues.

She ended our conversation with this comment. "You are a very good technician and leader, but don't think that it will be enough to keep you here. Understand the politics at play if you expect to survive."

I've never forgotten these words, and neither should you! You can be the best at your function, but if you are not aligned with your peers and support their business needs, you will not survive. When I say "business needs" – read "political agendas" – what does this person strive for, the CEO slot? Are they seeking the next higher position, a new position within the organization, or professional acclaim and notoriety? It's important to understand what drives those you work with, beyond the stated business objectives. What political faction are they aligned with, and how does that fit with your own sense of survival?

There are positional leaders, and then there are leaders via influence. The leaders via influence are the ones most likely to have agendas and those are likely to be political. This is not always bad if movement is in the best interest of the organization. If movement is self-serving then you might have a problem. Staying neutral is not always easy and not always the best course of action.

When I joined the organization as the IT Manager, I was not told that one of my staff had been turned down for the position, nor did I know that he ran the company golf league and was instrumental in finding donations for the annual golf tournament – everyone liked him. I still would have taken the job but with a better view on my challenges. I was also not aware of some of the nuances of assigning workloads via seniority as opposed to getting the job done with the available resources. Again, politics came into play for me when a subordinate refused to perform a function and said it "was not his job." My response as the manager was that it was all of our jobs to correct an outage – and didn't care whose job it was: "just let's get it done."

CISOs will have a higher level of politics because the stakes are higher, the turf more important, the risks are greater, and the organization can suffer a bigger impact if politics get in the way of the organization's success – and they have!

CISOs are often viewed as the impediment to a business function effort or an IT obstacle. In the past, that was often the situation – we were the department of "NO." Today, we have learned that politically it is not prudent or beneficial to say "NO." We must say, "How can we make that work with the existing policies of the organization?" or "How can I help you be successful and meet your goals?" Remembering that success for the business function is success for the CISO function as well, is key.

Compromise is a critical skill that will serve a CISO well when navigating into the political waters of an organization. Be quick to learn the political factions, and why and how they exist. Often politics are part of the organizational culture and might be difficult to understand, but politics exist in every organization – learn to identify the players and the agendas, try to map those to organizational success and accomplishment.

The Best Job/The Worst Job You Will Ever Have

I've said this many times to mentees, clients, and students. The CISO job is the best job you will ever have and it's the worst job you will ever have! This depends on a whole raft of issues, but YOU, the CISO, get to determine how you feel about the position.

It's the best job because you are engaged in many things and they change daily. Your environment changes, there is always an opportunity to learn, and the technology is always ready to challenge you. If you are performing your functions correctly, you are working with business owners, setting strategic plans, and validating the implementation and value of your tactical response activities. A viable CISO has a grasp on all activities that are going on within the organization – from new applications to Business Continuity Management. You are informed on planned infrastructure changes and planned enhancements, as well as potential partnerships that may lead to external connections into the environment.

A CISO must have an understanding of the future needs of the organization, as well as the skills to leverage current technology for additional value – unintended value previously not projected. An example of this would be to use Data Loss Prevention to catalog and embargo documents not ready to be shared. This is becoming more common today but sometimes we buy tools with tunnel vision and it takes an innovative CISO to move outside the "tunnel" and find a value add!

You are engaged with the executives of the organization (if you are not one) or sitting with your peers to make long-term business plans and decisions that impact many lives – employees, stakeholders, and customers. You are helping support the efforts that are being planned for organizational success and your function's effort will be involved in the operationalization of those plans and implementation of the controls to keep the organization protected from advisories and internal missteps.

You are at the forefront of the organization, expressing the organization's current capability to move in the planned direction and what resources will be needed in making the plans a reality, following all laws, regulations, policies, and processes while articulating the technical controls required.

This is the worst job you will ever have because you are always the point of the spear for defending the organization. It's your protection policies that are to blame when the organization is compromised! It's your staff that failed in their jobs to protect the organization from data exposure and unauthorized system manipulation. Your organization failed to protect the company from itself through misconfigurations or unauthorized changes.

I was chastised once by the CIO for an application getting into production resulting in the exposure of 7800+ credit card PII records being exposed. When I was asked how did "I" miss this issue, my response was simple – the application in question had been denied the Authorization to Operate (ATO), so it could not have possibly been running in production. Investigation revealed that the business owner VP ordered the application implemented outside the approval process. While I was not responsible for the actual issue, I was held accountable for not informing the CIO that the system had been denied the ATO, although the system notice had occurred. When the full After-Action exercise was completed, it found that the CISO function had followed all procedures and was not responsible for the data exposure; however, the organization was impacted at the customer level, having to provide credit monitoring to customers for three years, incurring an additional expense on the part of the company.

The CISO position is the worst, in that you may be put in the position of having to defend the organization from itself. For example, you often act as the mediator between competing business functions looking to make changes that affect others, without an agreement with the other party. Using a business owner's data without approval is often seen as controversial, telling a different story with the same data will start a turf war. CISOs can get into situations where there is a no-win outcome, they have to absorb the damage and move on – that is not easy for many CISOs, since our human nature is to fight the injustice being heaped on the function and on us.

A CISO that is well engaged in the business can aspire to any position in the organization, by understanding how the organization works, why it works that way, who makes it work – this is worth as much as any executive's skill. CISOs must be competent at all levels, know the laws and regulations (including global), policies, privacy issues, data protection issues, infrastructure and associated challenges, be familiar with new emerging technology and how it might benefit the organization, and how to leverage existing security tools to maximize value and longevity in the best interest of the organization and not themselves. CISOs must measure risk in doing something as well as not doing something, and find a balance that meets the organizational risk tolerance and appetite.

A CISO should always remember the three core elements of the role: identify risk or threat; articulate the impact of the risk or threat being exercised; and provide the best mitigation options/strategy for limiting or eliminating that impact. A CISO is not the final acceptance arbitrator, there are four options for the senior executives to take: accept the risk; mitigate the risk (using the CISO recommendation); eliminate the risk (stop the work); or transfer the risk to others – insurance and outsourcing. In most organizations, the CISO has no vote in the decision, BUT is a trusted resource in providing information for management to make the best decision.

The CISOs job is the best you will ever have, if you are ready to do the following: have the highest level of integrity and honesty, work hard, learn and grow your knowledge continuously, surround yourself with people smarter than you and trust them, fend off attempts at being bullied, experience reputational damage when things go wrong, and have your integrity questioned. You must be the face of calm in raging incidents and supporting the organization and your team 24/7/365.

The CISOs job does not start at 8 a.m. and end at 5 p.m.; it is 24/7. The threats keep coming and people make mistakes. This job is NOT a job for the faint of heart, but it could be the best one for you, if you have what it takes.

About the Author

Chuck McGann is currently the COO of The McGann Group, a small security consulting LLC in Raleigh, NC. He is a former CISO for the U.S. Postal Service, retiring in late 2014 (27 years of service) and moved on to the private sector as a VP and Chief Security Strategist for CRGT and then Salient CRGT. He started The McGann Group, LLC in 2017. Chuck's focus is to educate potential and current security professionals through his affiliation with EC_Council and Learning Tree International, delivering multiple courses for senior leaders and practitioners. Having spoken at numerous conferences and workshops, he continues to help grow the profession and educate the next generation of risk managers and security leaders in the skills needed for success. He holds an MBA, from Strayer University and undergrad degree from the University of Massachusetts in Computer Science and Management, and two associate degrees. His certifications include the CISSP, C|CISO, CISM, and IAM certificate. Chuck and his wife Mary Ann enjoy traveling, outdoor sports and camping, and family time (3 grown children). Chuck enjoys playing ice hockey for exercise and stress relief.

LinkedIn Profile

Chapter 2.1

THE POWER OF PRAGMATISM

By Jason Taule

As a 30+-year veteran of what we now call cyber security, I have had the infinitely good fortune to work with and for some of the most risk-minded organizations and supportive boards; and without a doubt, I owe much of my success to the talent and dedication of the teams with whom I've had the privilege to work. However, as something that, upon reflection, I now realize was both an advantage and disadvantage, I did not have the benefit of a CISO mentor – mostly because the position of CISO didn't yet exist and I was blazing a trail where few had gone before. Moreover, lacking mentors to whom I might go for guidance, I was compelled to seek answers from unusual sources and adapt traditional approaches in novel ways, which in the end, I firmly believe is one of the reasons I succeed where so many who are formally trained in "security" continue to struggle. My hope is that in sharing a few of the keys to my success, others may benefit accordingly.

Before digging in, I would like to take a moment to express my tremendous appreciation to and admiration for today's CISOs. Regardless of their exact title, the men and women responsible for managing the risks to which their organizations, their information assets, and their customers' data are exposed, are nothing short of heroes. Their task is complex and time consuming, requires a nearly impossible level of coverage, is plagued by backward looking and imperfect information, must yield positive changes in culture without hampering the business, and must be applied to a constantly evolving landscape with a limited set of resources. Not only, therefore, is it amazing that these individuals take on such jobs at all, but the fact that they do so with passion, integrity, and in most cases prevail, is nothing less than extraordinary.

What thoughts do I have to share? Regardless of whether you are a newly minted security/risk executive or a battle-hardened warrior with years of experience, I suggest we all would do well to consider the following five defining principles as guides for our actions:

- Forget the word security
- Pick a Framework
- Enable the business
- Empower your people
- The Board needs your help

Forget the Word Security

Many of us, myself included, have the word "security" in our title, and for good reason as that helps distinguish our role from that of other key executives. Beyond that, however, in my experience the term security is confusing at best, nebulous at worst, and should be dropped in favor of more useful terms to describe the role we play and the mission we serve.

Before considering alternatives terms, let us consider why the term security is troublesome. What does it even mean for an organization or the information assets upon which it depends to be secure? Can something be partly secure or is the concept binary? Consider what it would take to secure a laptop. It would have to be disconnected from all network connections, unplugged from its power source, powered down, locked up, housed in a protected enclosure, and put under the continuous watch of a guard. Is it now secure? Impossible to say; but what I do know for certain is that this asset has now been rendered completely useless.

Security is about risk and in putting assets to use we expose them by default to differing levels of risk and the question really is how to balance said exposure with the needs of the business. To clarify my meaning, as a CISO, you should talk about the matters of concern in terms of risk. Why? Because risk is the language of business. The men and women who run today's companies make business decisions every day and whether they are conscious of it or not, they do so based on risk. In fact, if you think about it, the C-suite is nothing more than an allocation of responsibilities consistent with the differing types of risks the entity faces: CFO? - Financial risk. Chief Counsel? - Legal risk. COO? - Operational risk. CCO? - Compliance Risk. CTO? - Technology risk. In this context, the job of a CISO is to help the organization manage its information risk.

This is not to say that as a CISO you do not need to have a technical background. In fact, I would argue just the opposite. There is no one model for a successful CISO and many professionals thrive in this role with diverse backgrounds, experiences, educations, and talent mixes. My point is merely that the successful CISO is often the one who can act as interpreter engaging directly with the organizations' technical staff to absorb issues and then express them with leadership in terms of the impact on the business. For example, senior leadership probably does not care to know how many outstanding network vulnerabilities you have identified or how many events per second your SOC is handling. Those things are the "what" but what they want to know about is the "so-what." So instead of focusing on security, evaluate for risk to which such issues expose the business. Then, it becomes a simple matter of communicating, ideally in quantifiable and/or financial terms, the impact to the business and its ability to achieve objectives of leaving such things untreated and what action(s) you recommend be taken.

Pick a Framework

Among the many and varied questions every CISO must answer, a few are universal and will be encountered regardless of company size, organizational complexity, business model, industry served, regulations faced, technology used, or types of information handled. For example, upon accepting the role of CISO, most individuals would immediately set about the task of understanding where the organization's current posture stands against its own objectives and mandated requirements and determining how best to achieve and maintain the desired end state; and this is exactly how it should be. Setting about answering these questions will serve you well as a CISO, but only to a point. There will come a time in every CISOs career when he or she will need to present to their board, and I can tell you from personal experience that no CISO wants to be faced with a question for which they do not have an answer. Had I the benefit of a CISO mentor, I might have learned the easy way that boards care less about having the "right" answer, than about the ability to defend the answer the organization chooses. This, of course, requires that as a CISO you can provide a "carefully reasoned and defensible response" to questions such as the following:

- What is our security, privacy, compliance, and risk current posture?
- How does that compare to where we need to be?
- What do our customers expect of us?
- How do we remain current with new laws, business models, and emerging threats?
- What is the proper level of resources to apply?

Admittedly, answering these questions initially and on a recurring basis is a large part of the CISOs job but if care is not exercised, this can consume an inordinate amount of the unwitting CISOs time. Even more critical than the efficacy with which a CISO addresses these matters is the need for credibility. Certainly, there are well educated, talented, experienced, highly respected, certified, and trusted CISOs whose expertise qualifies them to provide good answers to these questions. Those credentials are no guarantee against compromise, impermissible use, and/or breach. Additionally, when the inevitable happens, the organization will want something more than one person's opinion and that something comes in the form of a security and privacy controls framework.

As the CISO for HITRUST, a leading information protection and standards development and certification organization, you might expect me to tout the benefit of controls frameworks (and recommend adoption of the HITRUST CSF framework, in particular) and you would be right, but not for the reason you might expect. I am not biased towards controls frameworks because of where I work; it is the other way around. Having benefited greatly throughout my career by adopting such frameworks, it was only natural that my career progression led me to my current company and role. When I began my career, there were no security frameworks at all and no one even thought about privacy. In the 1980s, there was the so-called "Rainbow Series" of computer security standards and guidelines published by the Department of Defense. As an analyst for a large management consulting firm, I was part of a team that used these as the basis for building the first electronic data processing systems security programs for several major cabinet level agencies of the U.S. government. Repeatedly, we were able to explain why we were proposing something for adoption by explaining the fit, purpose, and value to the defense sector and its analog benefit to the civilian agency's mission and it is this same defensibility that leading frameworks offer now.

So, when your board asks you how you know that what your organization is doing is right or is enough, you can respond by saying that you adopted and aligned your practices with those encapsulated in the controls of the framework put forth by a leading standards development organization. Moreover, the same response will serve you well following a security event when you must explain yourself to your customers, regulators, stockholders/stakeholders, and to the public.

To a certain extent, any of the leading frameworks will do, but to be credible you should consider the following criteria when choosing which is the best fit for your organization. Specifically, the framework you select should:

- Be maintained by a recognized, accredited, and well-respected organization
- Provide guidance and controls for both security and privacy risks
- Cover your full breadth of operations across applicable industries and geographies
- Define control responsibilities for on-premise, cloud, and hybrid workload deployments
- Reflect the many regulations to which the organization is subject

- Offer automated capabilities to provide efficiencies
- Be publicly available for free to qualified organizations
- Be transparent and independently certifiable

Lastly, by adopting a controls framework you will realize one additional major benefit. In this global information-driven economy of ours, few if any organizations operate independently. Instead, most participate in and exchange data with a network of customers, trading partners, suppliers, and other third parties in an extended and interconnected ecosystem, such that the risk decisions that one party makes affects all the others. Adopting the right framework provides participants with a common means by which to readily obtain from and provide assurances to all others in the most effective manner possible.

Enable the Business

Security and privacy are no longer esoteric concerns but have risen to the point of mainstream awareness, such that organizational success now depends primarily on two things: access to capital and access to customers. Both objectives of course are dependent on confidence and trust. Investors only back organizations they are confident will provide a return. Likewise, fully aware that business transactions frequently necessitate exchange of sensitive information and/or systems interconnectivity, customers and trading partners are increasingly reluctant to do so with organizations who fail to respect their concerns about data security and privacy. Fortunately, many organizations recognize this and invest in information protection and compliance programs to meet their needs. The challenge, of course, is that rarely do organizations exist in isolation, which mandates conversation among parties and provision of assurances, to ensure the risk decisions an organization makes for its own purposes are equally well suited to the needs of those with whom they exchange information.

The point is that the matters to which a CISO devotes time and energy today are very different from the preoccupations of the past few decades. As awareness of the need for security and privacy has grown, organizations responded by increasing their investments. But, like everything else the company spends money on, there are resource constraints and a need to realize a benefit from the spend. For this and other reasons there is a trend, such that the traditional day-to-day work of "security" is becoming commoditized and gradually automated, with responsibility for delivery increasingly being assumed by the IT department, managed security providers, and/or the major cloud providers.

So, with IT and CSPs operationalizing an increasing part of the "security stack," what does that leave for the CISO to do? Plenty, at least for those CISOs who understand that their job is about managing risk and enabling the business. In fact, during interviews for various trade magazines and/or online security forums, I am often asked, "What keeps me up at night?" "What threat is my biggest concern?" or some variant on this question. My response is always the same: "people." I am a pragmatist not a cynic and I believe that most people are well intended and are simply trying to do their jobs. The challenge is that given the frenetic pace at which we are compelled to operate, one careless mistake can be the difference between the ability to devote time to strategic pursuits and an unwelcomed time commitment required by an incident response.

So, what is a CISO to do? Engage the business, of course. Get out of your office. Meet with your line of business owners. Find out what they need to do to succeed. Figure out where risk needs to be addressed in the key workflows of the business, anticipate those demands, and build processes to deliver what is needed without unwanted delay. In doing this you will quickly realize that the CISOs job is more about changing culture than changing technology. Moreover, to do this you need to learn to say "Yes, but…" rather than "No."

Consider a real-world example. One day you get a call from one of your company's SVPs who has been approached by a strategic partner with an opportunity that could benefit both organizations financially. The partner would like you to sell them data captured within systems you develop and host on behalf of third-party customers. By applying various data analytics techniques your partner is confident they could produce meaningful operational insights that would be of great value to the individuals and organizations involved. There is just one small problem. The data is Protected Health Information (PHI), you are a Covered Entity, and HIPAA specifically prohibits you from selling this data. Your response is a hard "no" right? Perhaps not. As a CISO, you should ask yourself "is there a way to get to yes?" Several options might come to mind. First, you could consider whether the pursuit would be possible with de-identified data. Alternatively, as a developer of software you may be allowed to use this data to make quality enhancements to your own software under the Privacy Rule which allows for certain uses and disclosures related to "Treatment, Payment, and Health Care Operations (TPO)." The point here is that risk is not black and white and, with a few rare exceptions, neither should your responses be.

Throughout my career I have served as CISO in a variety of organizations ranging from large publicly traded multi-nationals to privately owned certified small businesses, working in both the government and commercial sectors, and in both regulated and unregulated industries. I can tell you that when it comes to culture, no two organizations are alike, and although it is essential that a CISO remain adaptable, there are a few approaches that have consistently served me well:

- <u>Operations Table</u> – Each organization calls it by a different name, but there is always an "operations meeting" at which near to mid-term operations of the organization are discussed and key tactical decisions are made. As a CISO, it is imperative that you have a seat at this table, and you need to invite yourself into the "room where it happens," explaining the benefit if it is not already obvious to your senior leadership team. Those other executives look at business operations through differing lenses, and they should remain free to do so unconcerned by their lack of security and privacy expertise, because you are there. Your role then is to listen to the business requirements, understand the objectives, and find a way to help the business achieve those ends without exposing itself to undue levels of risk. What if the company wants to migrate away from its own data center into the cloud? No worries. You will take care of vetting the CSP, establishing an agreed-upon distribution of shared responsibilities, and binding them to terms according to your needs. How about when the company wants to increase revenue by expanding operations into a new country or industry sector? Again, no problem. You will take care of identifying and reporting back on your existing ability to meet the information security and compliance requirements with information about what it would take to address any gaps. You get the idea.

- <u>Customer/Partner Expectations</u> – Almost every organization is challenged by resource constraints that limit the number of strategic pursuits in which they can invest at any one time. As a CISO, you need to ensure that the "security function" is not seen as a tax on operations, but instead as something that contributes to the bottom line. What is the best way to do this? Alignment with the business is the answer most often given. However, that is something easier said than done. My recommendation is that you engage your customers and partners, find out what they expect of your company and what assurances they require as a condition of doing business with you, and then make delivery on these demands a core part of your program. As an example, in my career I served as the CISO for several different software development companies. First, as a federal systems integrator, I knew that the systems we were developing for agencies of the U.S. government were subject to FISMA and would be required to undergo a Certification and Accreditation (C&A) process as a condition of earning their Authority to Operate (ATO). I therefore made certain that my team was actively partnering with customer facing teams to craft all of the necessary security artifacts needed while also working with our internal IT department to ensure that the results of any scans would be in accordance with customer expectations. On the commercial side, I knew that customers would have questions of us about the posture of the software we were delivering as well as the hosted environment into which they would be expected to post their data. I therefore anticipated these demands and deployed an application security program to scan for and remediate code weaknesses, engaged a third party to perform external and internal penetration tests, and sought and obtained independent third party security certification. As CISO, the goal was to make it as easy as possible for our customers to do business with us and the ability to cite specific customer demands proved to be a highly effective way to justify spending requests.

- Service Catalog – Success in most things often comes down to communications and expectations management. Most business owners do not think about security and risk the way you do as a CISO, and that is okay. What you want to avoid is creating frustration when they do come to you with a request that you cannot fulfill in the time remaining. Are they to be blamed for not affording you more time? Perhaps. Ask yourself if you did everything you could to avoid the problem. Did you help foster a culture of mutual accountability by publishing a service catalog and educating your leadership about the services you will provide to them as your internal customers, explaining that to be timely you need a certain amount of lead time if they expect to hold you accountable? Do you have processes to support these asks? Are they automated? Are there self-service options? Don't think like a compliance analyst; instead, behave like the CEO of "Getting-to-Yes Inc."

- Hooks – By having a seat at the table, making it well known how and when to engage you and your team, and delivering the services as promised, a CISO will go a long way to promoting a culture of risk-mindedness. However, as the adage goes, no plan survives first contact with the enemy. In other words, regardless of how hard you work or how well you design and implement your procedures, things will go awry. People forget, emergencies arise, new people are hired, operations change, etc. So, you would do well to create so-called "hooks" that keep things from falling through the cracks. By hooks, I mean that as a CISO you should reach out to the heads of each corporate service team in your organization (i.e., Human Resources, IT, Help Desk,

Purchasing, Contracts, Facilities, Legal, etc.) with a simple ask that they refrain from signing-off on, approving, or otherwise fully processing selected requests if you have not yet provided your concurrence as CISO. Of course, this is something for which automated workflow is indicated, but the idea here is to ensure that you can help inform the decision relative to the information risk involved. I think you may be surprised to learn how receptive many of your peers are. In fact, and I say this tongue in cheek, but I know many CFOs who seek to limit organizational spending and love nothing more than to reject a purchase request putting the "blame" on security.

As a CISO, you should also be receptive to feedback from the other leaders in your organization and adapt accordingly, which brings me to the question of personal integrity. I said previously that there are some rare exceptions in which a hard "No" may indeed need to be the answer given. When and if that is a response you need to provide, is up to each person to decide. I have been fortunate never to have found myself in a situation that caused me to resign, because the organization I served sought to do something so egregious that I could not be party to it. But, it is vital that I make something clear, especially to those newly minted CISOs out there, and that is that this does not mean you will always agree with every business decision the company makes, and that is entirely acceptable. You see, your job is not to make the decision, but rather to ensure that your leadership team is fully apprised of the most current and accurate information, so that they can make the best decision possible. Businesses choose to accept risk every day and it is entirely within their purview to do so, provided they reach the conclusion in good faith. What you want to avoid is the unwitting acceptance of risk by your organization by default, owing to a lack of awareness of its existence or a proper appreciation for its significance.

Empower Your People

In the preceding section, I indicated that promoting a culture of security or risk-mindedness is what a CISO should be all about. This is most assuredly the case, but I want to make sure that readers do not mistakenly devote all their time to senior leadership at the expense of everyone else in their organization. "Culture eats strategy for breakfast" is a business maxim attributed to noted management consultant Peter Drucker. Nowhere is this truer than with respect to security and risk management. A CISO can have the best tech, the most robust budget, the most supportive leadership, and the most talented team, but none of that will matter if people click before they think.

I suggested earlier that those of us assuming the mantle of CISO should have our heads examined, and in large part that is because of the impossible nature of the job. To be successful, all a bad actor needs to do is find a single weakness to exploit; and most often that comes in the form of a person who clicked a spurious link in an email without realizing the harm they just created. Worse yet, is that many of these bad actors are social engineers (i.e., what we used to call con men) who prey on the fears workers have of getting in trouble for not following orders. Technical solutions (anti-malware, anti-spam, email sandboxes, DKIM, DMARC, email rules, intrusion detection, etc.) abound, but if you will pardon the pun, none are 100% foolproof. Instead, what you need to do as a CISO is to let your people know that you have their back. They need to understand that far from getting in trouble, you want them to check if they are not sure about something. If someone is yelling and screaming at them to do something, they need to understand that there is no place for such behavior in the work place, and that instead of worrying about the consequences, you will take the customer service "hit." By that I mean that you should have them respectfully explain to whomever it is that is directing them to do something about which they're not 100% certain, that they're sorry, they cannot do what is being asked, and that they will reach out to you (or your support team) and get back to them promptly with an answer. "When in doubt, check it out" is the mantra that wins the day! All told, you need to let your people know that you would infinitely prefer that they contact you (or your support team) with respect to something you already know about, or that turns out to be no big deal, than the other way around.

You also need to make sure that everyone understands that it is perfectly okay to contact you (or your support desk) at any time, and for any reason; and yes, this means even at zero-dark early in the morning on a Sunday. Furthermore, you need to emphasize that you really mean this because it is more likely that someone will attempt unauthorized access when people are not in front of their computers (which are typically left on and connected). Remind them that cyber is the new theater of economic warfare amongst companies and governments across the globe, who are in competition with one another, and that nation state-sponsored actor's attacks are directed to target certain assets as their day job working from one side of the world to the other, while you and your employees are fast asleep.

There are many ways to promote risk-minded behavior in an organization. Posters, emails, contests, rewarding good behavior with gift cards, security quizzes with company swag as prizes, anti-phishing exercises, and the like all come to mind. I cannot prescribe for you exactly what methods you should use to foster a risk-minded culture; however, I encourage you to experiment and try whatever works, and share your results with others. What I can offer is a quick test you can use to determine whether you have succeeded. Specifically, ask yourself if someone in your organization witnessed someone else doing something wrong, would they:

1. Know that it is wrong?
2. Choose to do something about it?
3. Know to whom and how to report it?

As simple as these three questions are to articulate, you may find it takes a surprising amount of time until you can answer yes to all three and do so on a continuous basis. It is vital that you keep at it, until you can do so for all situations for which you are responsible, as anything less means you still have work to do.

Properly Engage Your Board

Having spoken about the role of and relationship between the CISO and senior leadership, corporate service peers, customers/trading partners, and the members of the organization's workforce, that leaves but one group to address – The Board. Best for last right? Let me know what you think when you have finished reading this section.

Hollywood often depicts a company's Board of Directors as a group of cigar smoking country club cronies who come together a few times a year to down a few martinis, enjoy a juicy steak, and pocket a fat check. Nothing could be farther from the truth. A seat on the Board of a company is not some sort of perk, but rather is a serious job with fiduciary responsibilities that comes with real liability. No longer are these individuals above the fray as the decisions and actions of these bodies are increasingly scrutinized by regulators, shareholders, and others. With respect to security, privacy, and risk, this means that the Board is expected to have concrete, accurate, and current answers to certain key questions and exercise appropriate levels of oversight, and that as Sherlock said to Dr. Watson, is something you can use to your advantage.

Ask any CISO and they will have a story to share with you about the first time they went before a Board of Directors. You will likely hear that these were tense presentations for which the person was not well prepared and that CISOs do not get much time on the agenda (or that it is a bad sign if a substantial portion of the agenda is devoted to matters of security). For the most part, these stories are accurate, but I am here to tell you that it need not be this way. A board meeting is an opportunity to be embraced, not a burden to be avoided, and if approached the right way, the Board can be a CISOs strongest ally. The difference is all in the expectations you set about, and who is responsible for what.

Many CISOs think of board meetings as the time to make a budgetary ask, where they will be challenged to make the case for every dollar sought, and where they will have to report on their lack of progress if they did not obtain all of the funding requested. They expect to be called "chicken little" because of the perceived necessity of painting a worst-case picture to justify funding. This is because these CISOs have unwittingly fallen into the trap of thinking that they are the senior-most person in the company charged with responsibility for security and risk. Despite what it may say on your job description, the CISO is not where the buck actually stops. When it comes to security and risk, the buck stops with the Board–nowhere else. Organizations like the Information Systems Audit and Control Association (ISACA), IT Governance Institute (ITGI), the National Association of Corporate Directors (NACD), and others have clearly established that it is the Board of Directors who is ultimately responsible for security, privacy, risk management, and governance.

So, what does this mean for you? It means that your task is not to go into the boardroom to ask them for funding. Instead, you should politely turn the tables. It is about you helping them understand what it is for which they are responsible and then extending an offer to help them fulfill those very obligations. Your job is to present to them a clear picture of the many security related activities for which the Board is responsible and ask them which items they would like your assistance with. It is up to them (with your guidance of course) to tell you which items they want to work on, in what order, and with what funding. Of course, you still need to address governance and are accountable to make the best use of limited resources, but at the end of the day it is the Board that makes decisions about what to invest in and what to defer, not you.

So, coming full circle, to properly engage the Board you'll want to create an executive level dashboard (I suggest that you do this in accordance with the controls framework you chose above) and use that as the mechanism by which to keep the Board regularly informed of the company posture, showing where it is relative to where it seeks to be (relative to its own internal risk appetite) and relative to where it is required to be (relative to the various mandates to which the organization falls subject). But, remember, it is about risk, so a mere gap by itself needs to be augmented by you with data to convey whether and to what extent a variance is a cause for concern. You can then, look to the Board for guidance on what to do and which initiatives they would like to fund.

      *   *   *   *   *

It is my sincere hope that in sharing these few ideas, I have helped others avoid the pitfalls that too often plague our industry and profession. And as much as I welcome the opportunity to learn of your accomplishments, it is more important to me that each of you "pay it forward" by finding others who might benefit from your mentorship. As Shakespeare said, "If it be not now, yet it will come, the readiness is all" and we are all in this together.

About the Author

Jason Taule

CCSFP, CMC, CPCM, HCISPP, CCISO, CISM, CGEIT, CRISC, CHSIII, CDPSE, CDPS, NSA-IAM

Jason Taule is a 30+-year information assurance and cybersecurity veteran who has worked in both the intelligence community and commercial sectors, first consulting to federal agencies and then serving as inside CISO and CPO both within the government and at large systems integrators like General Dynamics and CSC.

Mr. Taule helped build the original DARPA CERT, helped develop the first computer security programs at the VA and NASA, and revised the Risk Assessment Methodology still in use throughout DHHS. Mr. Taule helped author the Maryland Data Privacy Law, led a multi-million dollar global cyber security practice for a large international consulting firm, ran the team responsible for HIPAA complaint investigations for OCR for 3 years, and for the last 20 years has been a luminary in the U.S. Health IT sector helping hundreds of systems earn their accreditations and avoid compromise.

Mr. Taule currently serves as HITRUST Vice President of Standards and Chief Information Security Officer (CISO). In this capacity, he oversees the ongoing development and evolution of the HITRUST CSF security and privacy controls framework to ensure its continued relevancy and sufficiency. This includes a broad range of HITRUST risk management framework support functions such as requirements integration, control specification, and the development of standards that organizations can use to develop their own information protection and compliance programs and provide assurances to customers, trading partners, and other third parties. Additionally, Mr. Taule oversees HITRUSTs internal information assurance efforts to ensure that the organization continues to earn and keep the confidence of customers and third parties who have entrusted HITRUST with the safekeeping of their data.

Mr. Taule holds a Master of Science in Information Technology Management from Johns Hopkins University and a Bachelor of Business Administration from the College of William and Mary. Mr. Taule has earned numerous industry and professional certifications, is a graduate of the FBI Citizen's Academy, a member of the Homeland Security Preparation and Response Team, serves on the Board of the Loyola Sellinger School of Business and the Howard County Economic Development Authority Technology Council, and is a founding member of and National Advisor to the CISO Executive Network. Mr. Taule sits on the DHHS/CMS Information Security and Privacy Workgroup, the FBI Cyber Health Work Group, the U.S. Health IT Standards Committee's Transport and Security Workgroup and is a White House invitee to the Security Policy Roundtable for the President's Precision Medicine Initiative.

LinkedIn Profile

Chapter 2.2

THE UNEXPECTED ROLES OF A SECURITY LEADER

By Jessica Nemmers

The fact that I am now a Chief Security Officer (CSO) was unexpected. You see, I was trained since the age of six to be a professional ballerina, and I had an amazing 7-year career. Unfortunately, my career ended unexpectedly due to a lack of funding for the ballet company. This was in 1996, and just as unexpected as my ballet career ended, my Information Technology career began.

My career path to becoming a CISO (and now CSO) looks very different from other security leaders I know. As I have collaborated with other successful security leaders, I discovered that we all have assumed roles that we never expected to be included with our job title. To clarify in my case, the difference between being a CISO and a CSO is overseeing physical security as well as information security (often called "cyber" security) as the title CISO suggests.

My "Leap" into IT

"How on Earth did you get into security from being a ballerina?" I hear this question often and the answer is that it is a bit of a complicated journey. My story demonstrates that a successful security leader does not have to come from a traditional cyber security background.

On March 5, 1996, all company dancers reported back to the studio after our day off from a great performance the weekend before. We were told not to "dress out" and to clean out our lockers and come back to the lounge for an emergency meeting. With tears in his eyes, our Artistic Director notified us that necessary funding for our non-profit ballet company had not come through and that they had no other option than to permanently shut our doors and declare Chapter 13 bankruptcy. With no warning, no severance, and no other ballet company in our city to hire me as a dancer, I went home wondering what I was going to do next.

Not long after the devastating news of our company closing, a friend who used to work for the ballet told me about an opportunity to work on the helpdesk for a $10M arts festival through a partnership with Hitachi and Electronic Data Systems (EDS). I bought a suit for the interview and met with the COO of the festival, who was on loan from the New York Shakespeare Festival. Guess what? He knew less about computers than I did, so I already had an advantage. He determined that I was overqualified to answer phones on the festival helpdesk and offered me the position as his assistant. Without much hesitation, I accepted the job.

Even though this was a Japanese Arts Festival, I began to learn important skills that I would use throughout the rest of my career. I also began to find the joy of working in Information Technology (IT). This was my leap into IT, and about a year later, I would walk into a Tier 4 data center and know that I wanted to be in security. I did not know exactly what the journey would look like, but almost 20 years later, would become a security leader and would build my first security program.

"You Need to Get Your CISSP"

It is common that security leaders often achieve their Certified Information Systems Security Professional (CISSP) certification. This is not focused on leadership but covers eight domains within the security realm (at the time of this book's publishing) and is known as the exam that is "a mile wide and an inch deep." My company made this a requirement when I became the Security Manager, so after a lot of studying, I took the exam and then finished the required documentation of my experience and the necessary endorsement to achieve full certification. I personally feel this is still a very relevant certification for anyone in cyber security. There is also the Certified Information Security Manager (CISM) certification that focuses more on leadership. Both certifications can support your ongoing skills as a CISO.

I learned a great deal about the technology behind security and important information to make decisions on my security program through my CISSP certification process. Once I began to build my security program at a $5B Fortune 500 company, I quickly realized that being an effective security leader requires you to assume roles that are often unexpected.

I will offer a word of caution as we begin to talk about the unexpected roles of a security leader. You will most likely find yourself getting further and further away from having the technical expertise of a Security Analyst or Security Engineer. That is okay, because being a CISO, CSO, or other security leader is a leadership role. Whether you are directly leading a team or leading the security function - you are a leader.

Unexpected Role Number 1: Leader

"What should I do to get to the next level?" This question often comes into the conversation during an annual performance review. Cyber security professionals tend to be hungry and want to climb the ladder. Just as you think you may finally have filled an open position on your team, the employee is offered another one that pays 30% higher. More and more we are faced with the ever-growing "Cyber Security Skills Shortage." The gap gets much wider when you receive a resignation from a star team member and remember that it took 6 months to fill the position the last time it was open.

As busy as you are with your security program, you are a leader in a field where there is not enough talent. Companies want the most talented security professionals to defend their company. It is important as a leader that you focus on taking care of the people on your team.

Some CISOs own a program with few or maybe no direct reports. You must still act as a leader of your program. Study how leaders build and foster relationships. Observe who your decision makers are and build relationships with them.

The technology of security is so cool, but if you are a CISO, your time should be focused on leading your team and program, and less on the scripts that your team is running as part of their ongoing threat hunting. Hire the smart people and lead them to success.

Unexpected Role Number 2: Influencer

Something I did not expect as a CSO is the amount of influence I must have to be successful in my job. Depending on how your program is aligned with the business and your IT department, your team may not do much of the actual work (we will talk about your role as "Governor" soon) to safeguard your company's resources and data.

One would think that most companies would see cyber as a major risk and therefore allocate a large security budget and an even larger security team to mitigate that risk, but that is not the case. Not only are we faced with small, often overworked teams, but the IT teams that support us are often operating very lean, as well.

There is at least one session of every security conference that I attend titled "Presenting to the Board." Business leaders, and even IT Leaders, often do not understand cyber security risks and what it takes to protect a company against a cyber-attack or data breach. CISOs often do not understand how to communicate cyber-related risk.

Your job as an influencer is to communicate such cyber-related risks to your stakeholders. You will need the support of the Board or Executives to fund your program and you will need time and staff from your IT department to install, configure, and run your security solutions. IT team members are key to your program's success whether it be to stand up a server to run your security tools or apply infrastructure and application patches. Your program's requirements are not their priority, but you must influence them to make it one, for your program to be successful.

Your influence as a CSO/CISO largely depends on how you are perceived within your company. Think about how others see you and your position. Are you the "Office of No" or the guy in the meeting trying to get your stakeholder's attention by telling frightening stories of cyber-attacks that have happened at other companies? Better yet, are you seen as a trusted advisor and business partner who has the company's best interest in mind and are willing to enable the business to operate securely?

As you move into a position as a security leader and gain a seat at the table with your executives and possibly the Board of Directors, it may be the perfect time to brush up on some books about influencing your business stakeholders. I also highly recommend working with an executive coach. No matter the size of your team, the size of the security risk is large. Your ability to influence stakeholders may be the difference between successfully managing through a cyber-attack and going out of business because of one.

Unexpected Role Number 3: Salesperson

As a CISO you will spend an extraordinary amount of time working (or dealing) with vendors. You will find some of your vendors become great personal friends, while others are folks that you will walk out of your way to avoid being looped into a conversation. These vendors need one thing from you: to sell their security solutions to you.

I could probably write another chapter on dealing with vendors, but we will leave that as a possible sequel to this book. One small piece of advice that has helped me along my journey is to partner with a great Value Added Reseller (VAR) and allow him/her to play block and tackle with the vendors so you are not spending too much of your valuable time listening to sales pitches. A good VAR will also handle the negotiation and payment terms with your procurement department when you are purchasing a new service or solution.

So, why as a CISO, do you need to be a salesperson? Well, you will need money for these latest and greatest solutions that are going to protect your company and give you the tools to assess cybersecurity risk. Once you have determined the most cost-effective solution for your risk mitigation strategy, your job will be to sell the solution to your stakeholders. This is of course, after you have built the relationships and the trust to help *influence* the decision.

If you have not taken sales training in the past, I recommend you do. Think "Shark Tank" when you are approaching your Board of Directors for a Multi Factor Authentication solution that costs $350,000 and will take five resources from the IT teams (and maybe two of yours) devoted over multiple weeks to get it implemented. That takes a great sales pitch.

Selling your security program is often quite difficult. Those who are funding your program may take the, "Well, it hasn't happened yet, so I think we are good" approach, which may or may not work out for you if you are the victim of a cyber-attack or data breach. You are often selling what feels like a fence in a backyard. How effective is your fence at home? Has it been a strong protection to you? What is your Return on Investment (ROI) on that fence for you and your family?

You might not be able to answer the fence investment questions until a small child comes into your backyard and falls into your swimming pool. Suddenly that fence may have prevented a disastrous outcome. As you assume the role of a CISO, get ready to practice your sales pitch until you can speak with facts and confidence.

A last thought on this topic is to refrain from scaring your audience. Security is a risk discussion and presenting alarmist "might happen" doomsday scenarios may cause your stakeholders, who you have influence over, to lose trust in your recommendations.

Unexpected Role Number 4: Trainer

At the beginning of my IT career, all I ever wanted to do was work in the datacenter. I loved the physical security aspect and the challenge of securing that much information in one place. As it turns out, it would be years until I could assume a full-time security position at a company. Apparently, my time on stage as a professional ballerina gave me the ability to stand up in front of large audiences without getting nervous. My company found my hidden talent in training and I soon became certified as a trainer and quickly a Global Training Manager.

I was so excited to be able to finally transition back into security after my training career, but guess what I have spent almost 30% of my time doing? Training!

As a CISO, you must have a strong security program. Vulnerability and Patch Management, Firewall Management, and Endpoint Protection are important facets of your program "to protect your company and reduce the risk of business disruption or brand damage due to a cyber related attack or data breach" (get used to saying this phrase; you will say it often).

Perhaps the most important facet of your security program is going to be Security Awareness and conducting Phish Testing with your employees. Yes, train your employees! Spend lots of time training your employees on how to recognize a phishing email, what do to when they have accidentally clicked on a phishing email, and how to notify your team if they see something suspicious happening. Humans are the greatest cyber related threat to your company. If you are not spending time training them, the millions of dollars spent on security solutions will not make any difference.

Unexpected Role Number 5: Author

Well, here I am writing a chapter in this book, so yes, I never thought I would be an "author," per se, yet I have authored many documents in my security career.

Just as you must have a succinct sales pitch when you are seeking funding for a new security solution or an additional team member, you should be ready to articulate reports, updates, alerts, and recommendations in written form. Even if you have a fantastic Corporate Communications team at your company, you will need to do most of the writing to ensure your point is clear.

As a CISO, when you author your works, it is crucial to stay away from the tech talk. Think like your audience and use analogies that will allow them to relate to the subject. For example, if you are speaking about access control, use people with keys to rooms in one home as an analogy to the concept of Role Based Access Control (RBAC).

Unexpected Role Number 6: Governor

No one ever told me that as a CISO, your team does not really "do" the work. Granted, every security team at every organization is different, but there are Separation of Duties (SOD) that exist to ensure security is not overreaching. You are the governor of security for the organization.

Governance, Risk, and Compliance (GRC) has taken on a very different role since major cyber related attacks began appearing on the news. Security is a company's risk, not a company's technology department. Compliance is crucial not only to give your partners or customers confidence in your program, but for many companies, it is a requirement to stay in business. Security controls exist to protect the company from damage resulting from a cyber-attack, but also to protect against heavy fines for perceived (or true) negligence.

Your role as a CISO is to ensure that the teams "doing" the work to protect the company are doing it by the book. An important piece of advice I received early into my first CISO role was "do not ever lie on an attestation that you have a certain security control." Why was I told this from my fellow CISO and trusted advisor? If your company is a victim of a cyber related attack and are looking to your cyber insurance company to cover the damage, they will refuse coverage if they find you have lied about your controls.

Be a good governor and ensure that compliance is met to the level that is stated and nothing less.

Roles that You Should Expect to Have: Business Partner and Trusted Advisor

Being a CISO is a blend of technology leader and strategist. With your roles of leader, influencer, salesperson, trainer, author, and governor, your goal should be to become your CEOs Business Partner and Trusted Advisor. Your executives should feel confident that each aspect of your program exists to support the business and align with the company's goals.

It is always a balance between keeping the company secure and allowing it to run freely. Many times, you will be met with difficult decisions about certain security configurations. You will have to weigh the risk of implementing the control that may break business operations, or not implementing and being left vulnerable to a cyber-attack.

Spending time with your stakeholders and truly understanding their business drivers, corporate goals, financial targets, and most of all, pain points, will arm you with important information to present your case when needed. Keep reminding yourself that the reason you are where you are is that they trust your guidance to get them where they want to go.

I wish you the very best of luck in your journey. Do not forget to reach out to members of your security community. Even a CISO needs trusted advisors. We will not defeat the cybercriminals unless we are working together.

About the Author

 Jessica Nemmers is the Chief Security Officer of Elevate Credit. As a CSO, Jessica focuses on building security programs that align with business objectives and compliance drivers to reduce the risk of business disruption, financial loss, or brand damage from a cyber-attack.

With over 24 years in the IT industry, Jessica began her career with Perot Systems (now NTT Data). At Perot Systems, Jessica led IT teams in the U.S., India, Romania, and Mexico, and was a founding member of Perot Systems Mexico. Jessica also held positions in new business development, data center operations, and IT communications, which allowed her to leverage her unique ability to translate technical solutions to non-technical audiences.

Prior to her role at Elevate, Jessica was with Commercial Metals Company (CMC) where she built a comprehensive security program from the ground up to protect critical systems on business and Operational Technology (OT) networks at more than 230 sites worldwide.

Jessica has been recognized for her work as a trailblazer in cyber security as an honoree of the 2020 Dallas Business Journal's Women in Technology Awards. She was also named as one of the 500 most powerful business leaders in North Texas by D CEO Magazine. Jessica holds a B.S.

in Business, HR Management, and is a Certified Information Systems Security Professional (CISSP).

Prior to her career in Information Security, Jessica was a professional ballerina and performed across the southern United States with her company. Almost 20 years after her retirement, both of her sons chose to study classical ballet. She is now a proud "dance mom" and loves watching her sons perform. Ryan (19) is a professional danseur with Colorado Ballet, while Ben (16) currently studies dance at Booker T. Washington School of the Performing and Visual Arts in Downtown Dallas.

LinkedIn Profile

Chapter 2.3

FROM THE CIO LENS
By Bryan Tutor

I'm honored to be amongst such prestigious information security professionals. I was asked to bring the Chief Information Officer perspective to this collection of CISO mentoring advice. My approach to this chapter is to provide the governing framework that the CIO brings to the discussion and how information security plays such a vital role in the business. Information Technology is often viewed as an "expense" to the business. The reality is that if you are not producing revenue – you are a cost of doing business – an expense.

The obvious business goal is to create a profit for our shareholders, so how can security be a cost and still be a value-added function? It's important to demonstrate value. There are many reasons why security is important, however the Chief Executive Officer has to determine where resources are applied and the CIO is the advisor to provide the compelling business case to obtain much needed resources, without creating a compromise to the rest of the business that needs resources for new products and customers.

Throughout my career, I have served in many capacities. My starting point was in Production Technology where we built specialized manufacturing equipment for the shop floor. This was rewarding, because I was able to achieve a sense of accomplishment by helping others do their job efficiently. Later I worked for the Vice President of Operations and learned the business ropes. I learned early on that you need to create a clear linkage to the Mission, Vision, Values, Objectives, and Tactics of the organization. Without the clear linkage, you will miss the mark with all future conversations with your CIO and CEO, as well as other business functions that are competing for resources.

My career led me afterwards into the Information Technology organization. My initial focus as an account manager drove me to alignment of business imperatives and IT implications. It was simple – if we were doing projects that did not align to the business imperatives, we stopped!

We did transformative projects that focused on making the business productive and profitable. The goal was to be known as a valuable contributor to the value stream. By doing so, you get a seat at the table and a voice. Getting there is one thing, staying there is another. Helping your CIO keep the required credibility and earning it daily will help them get the necessary resources that are essential for maintaining secure business operations.

The digital pivot we have all had to make through the 2020 pandemic, has taken us to heightened levels of security in all regards. With all things digital, there are no walls. Yes, firewalls exist, but they are only as good as the weakest link or setting in any case.

No one can really survive a digital breach. It's painful in every way. It undermines the credibility of the company and those running it. NO pressure! The main way I look at risk management is to look at all the knowns that we can fix, understand where we may have weaknesses that can be mitigated and then remain as paranoid as possible, to ensure that we don't get complacent.

How many leaders sleep with their phone on the nightstand next to the bed? Most do. That's what we do. When the call comes in, we have to respond. Whenever I got these nighttime calls, I would clear my voice (as if I had been waiting for it) and I would prepare to respond with readiness and alertness.

Stuff does happen, large or small. As a leader, you will have to communicate clearly and quickly. Bad news is not like cheese, it does not get better with age. Acting decisively and informing the chain of command with all of the "knowns" is the appropriate immediate action. You will not have all the answers at the onset, so do not speculate or provide excuses or try to "spin" things in any way. Get the help that you need and act, demanding that all hands be on deck.

CISO Character

The CISO position requires resiliency. It takes special characteristics to perform this often-thankless position. When everything is going well, you are unnoticed, and from my experience, that is the preference. However, when disasters occur, you can't just decide to take a break. You know this is often the Wednesday before the Thanksgiving Holiday, or just before that long-awaited vacation that you desperately needed. Sorry! The CISO has to be on point 24/7, or at least have a team, process, and tools that will be ready to defend and protect the assets at all times. Your CIO and CEO appreciate the persistence and drive to defend the digital keys of the enterprise.

Your role is valued by the enterprise. Your job is to be pessimistic, paranoid, watchful, and open to the needs of the business. If you are overly vigilant, you will impair the ability of the business to maintain the necessary agility to meet the competitive demands of the business. It's all about finding the appropriate balance. This is where having an open communication with the CIO is an imperative. You both have needs and you have to understand each other's requirements, so that you can strike the right balance between both sides. This is especially needed during a crisis, which statistically should happen with a fair amount of frequency.

Don't panic!

Everyone is watching how you handle the situation, including your peers, superiors, and your employees. How you react will determine their actions, in your favor or against you. If you are hunting for someone to blame, then everyone will hide, and you will never get to the root cause of the incident or breach. It is your responsibility to create an environment where everyone feels "safe" to bring issues forward, and where they will know that you will be fair and act with justice. This is something you build in advance, well before the time an issue occurs. Your objective is to foster trust.

When you have an issue, be prepared to dissect it and fully understand what happened. I had the opportunity to obtain a Six Sigma Green Belt from the University of Michigan. We studied and learned the Root Cause and Corrective Action methodology, and the most useful tools to me where the "5-Whys" and the Fishbone diagram.

I was managing a large production contract and we encountered quality issues that required a deep level of understanding of what had happened. We dug deeply into the questions of the situation, and we took an approach that considered that anything could have happened, while putting it into the framework of the 5-Why's. We learned how amazing it is when you break down the issue into non-defensive statements, and just lay it all out there for review, and then test the information and data that is presented. This requires that you truly open up and investigate thoroughly the objective evidence. Interviewing everyone involved is also a critical step in this process; whereby, once again, the environment of trust and openness is key to success.

Sometimes (most of the time) there are issues beyond your control!

As leaders, we manage variables. We have to understand the big picture and work the fringes. When you do an audit, it covers the basics. You have to dig beyond that and understand the bigger questions of where threats may be hiding. It goes back to what you know, what you should have known, and that into which you had no visibility. Our job requires us to focus on the second one: what you should have known, and here is a way of breaking down that question into smaller areas:

1. How can you get to what you should have known?
2. How do you react when surprised?
3. How often do you regret what you have said?
4. How can you prepare for every question coming at you?
5. What deer-in-the-headlight questions have you had?
6. When have you been caught flat-footed when you should not have?
7. When have you thought you covered all grounds and you didn't?

Navigation is a key element of leadership. You need to know the mission and the direction the business is moving; otherwise, you will create friction and frustration that does not help either party.

Spending time with leadership will help you understand how to best align with them. If you skip this step, it will be difficult to recover. You should know that this is not difficult; simply engage the emotional skills you already have and get on the same level of understanding with them. Some of those leaders will 'get' you and some will not, so you will have to learn to decide how much time you spend with each group, in order to move the relationships forward.

Sometimes you don't get to choose whom you engage with and you have to navigate these situations as well. Know the abilities as well as the limitations of those who surround you. Not everyone is a superstar at everything, which is why the leader has to "orchestrate" the strengths and shore up the weaknesses within the team. Being a coach and cheerleader is a very necessary part of what the leader does.

I can't overemphasize the need for trust within the team. It is between you and each member of the team as well as creating that teamwork bond between each other. Watch for agendas and do not allow them to permeate this hard-earned fabric of trust you have formed. I've had the opportunity to lead some phenomenal teams. What made them amazing was how well everyone worked together for the greater mission.

People First - No Boundaries

I like to see people rewarded for their passion, so I try to encourage people to find what their passion is and help them get there. "No Boundaries" to me means that we don't want to limit people's potential. If we limit (via boundaries) then we run the risk of losing their engagement. When someone is engaged with the business, they will be more productive, and this passion fuels the enterprise.

When I began working at my most recent position, I conducted simple surveys once a quarter to understand how engaged the Information Technology organization was. Any response was taken seriously, whether they were happy or not, as my first consideration was to look for people to have an opinion. Those that chose not to respond at all became a big concern for me. I wanted people to express something that would allow me to act upon it. It is worth pointing out that surveys can also be dangerous, since there is an expectation of subsequent action. If you don't act on the responses, they won't respond again in the future, and you lose credibility.

Not everyone gets to choose their role and be passionate about everything that they do. I believe we should do what we can to help mentor and coach employees in that direction, to the extent that we can do so. Sometimes the passion just cannot be fueled, and when this takes place, you have to make hard decisions for the betterment of the organization.

No Friction

The Information Technology organization touches every part of the business. All things are digital and that is how work is accomplished in today's environment. To that end, we need to ensure that we are easy to work with. I like to talk to my teams about being an "IT Friendly" organization that does not create friction for the business. We are here to serve the business functions by providing reliable and timely solutions and services.

Sources of friction can stem from "old school IT" attitudes that manifest themselves in ways that come across as if IT knows it all. Today, everyone is an expert in IT. Being overly bureaucratic does not help things either. I've heard too many times that if you define your requirements then it is easier to deliver. When new initiatives arise, and if IT is the primary expert amongst various parties, then sit with your customers and help them define the requirements (I was always able to start with the back of a napkin).

By reducing friction, we can help the business operate more efficiently and effectively. I've gotten feedback from other CIOs on the nightmares of getting all of the new employee's technology needs in-place in a timely manner. We initiated a program a few years back that I referred to as the "IT Concierge" program. It was designed to help on-board new employees with their technology needs. This is something that I am very passionate about. Hearing from a business unit that it took days or weeks to get an employee productive, is completely unacceptable. Our goal became the following: everything is in-place before the employee arrives. A tangential benefit was that the employee felt valued, and this leads back to fostering greater engagement. An employee that feels valued is more likely to be an engaged employee. The total benefit includes better retention, better place to work, and more likely, that the employee will tell others about how great it is to work for a company that cares.

Another benefit of being an "IT Friendly" organization is that fewer shadow groups are formed. Shadow groups can create security risks by not following the appropriate protocols. Once they pop up, it takes wasted efforts to get things back under control. Being a partner to the business and staying engaged with the business functions will limit shadow activity. Since all things are digital, it's impossible to serve every digital need from the formal IT group, and sometimes it is better to partner with business functions and enable and guide them, in order to keep information safe, and to get the projects done that are necessary to foster innovation and keep the business moving forward.

Product successes are typically seen through a speed to market cycle. Technology projects are the same. Providing an 85% solution in two weeks is better than an 88% solution in two months. Your technology consumers will appreciate the faster turn-around and view you as an enabler versus an inhibitor, making you feel good about helping the business.

Create the Environment to Excel

Whether you are a CIO or CISO or are in any other leadership position, it is your responsibility to create the environment for the team to be successful. I've observed CISOs that are so stretched thin that it projects and translates to stress in those who are under their leadership. When this is happening, you have to step back and recalibrate the big picture. Identify what is creating the "stretch." This is where it helps to whiteboard and identify the "stressors" of all the knowns and the unknowns. However, watch out, because doing this exercise could also lead to more stress. Personally, I would rather know what to be stressed out about than to be surprised about something I do not know.

Once you identify the stressors, you can develop an action plan. I would prefer to be in the middle of building an action plan, than have something happen that we were completely unaware of. Getting caught "flat-footed" is not good for anyone. Keeping surprises away will also lead to stress reduction and more likely to greater job longevity.

How Can I Help?

Since this book is mostly about CISO successes, I wanted to change gears here at the end of this chapter. The CISO role has many dimensions similar to the CIO role. If the CISO role falls under the CIO or CTO role, then for the CIO, the CISO is only one of several dimensions. I had a great discussion with my former CISO about how he could help me more. He realized that when he brought too much stuff to me, I would get lost in the details. I never meant to be rude, so I once said "I want to know what time it is, not how to build the clock." I caught him off guard, since he had never heard that before.

There is ownership on both sides of the fence between the CIO and CISO. There were many things that, as the CIO, I did not need to know regarding specific details on an investigation or other items. This was my CISOs role to work with Legal or Corporate Security to resolve. My CISO recognized this and limited what I really needed to know, and this was very much appreciated by me. The other side of this is to make sure that there is a clear understanding that you can't limit the information too much. This is quite the balancing act. Information that is too watered down is not usable.

The question for you, the reader, is this: how do you determine the balance described above? Do you under or over feed your CIO, assuming that is the reporting relationship? What is the formula for the right balance of information?

A suggestion would be to develop a list of all projects or even the "stressors" that were mentioned earlier and sit down to discuss these together. It would be good to come in with your view of priorities and risks and difficulty to solve. It doesn't matter if you are right or wrong, it creates a healthy conversation. Once you have done this, together you can share a certain amount of responsibility. The CIO needs to take the priorities and determine how this aligns with overall business risks and priorities. To be clear, this is not a release of responsibility to continue to be vigilant, but just an "airing" of the concerns and an avenue to build a plan going forward - together.

Concluding Thoughts

We started with a discussion of aligning our priorities to the business imperatives. This is fundamental. Each of you has had career successes and failures, that's your backdrop. That's also what put you where you are. Use your history as learning experiences that will help propel you in the future. This book is a great collection of experiences from your peers that we can all benefit from. I have learned from everyone I've worked with. Some of the experiences have been challenging. We are sharpened by our trials. Learn from your experiences as well; those that are good and those that are bad. Taking those experiences to a level of understanding that allows you to improve your team is what leadership is all about.

A thankless job

As you already know, the CISO role is thankless, but many positions are in the same boat. Don't underestimate your value in the organization. Truly, you are valued! The CIO, or whomever you are reporting to, has many demands and recognizes the value of the CISO function. Remain vigilant in your command and keep everyone informed of what the risks are and how we can best address them. The CISO position must be unwavering, persistent, consistent, and you cannot tire easily. Sounds like a super hero – go with that!

At this point in my career, I really enjoy the ability to tell my team something like this: "That's not hard; I've seen hard!" Being confident based on your experiences is okay - being arrogant is not! Be confident, but humble, above all - be a great leader!

Targeted Advice for Those Aspiring to Be a CISO

You are a special breed. It takes passion and perseverance to do this role. I've seen people that have a desire to do this but when the glamour is not so glamorous, they go in a different direction. This is ok. Search deeply and make sure you have the right elements to succeed. There is a lot of responsibility in this role and, as I said earlier, when something bad happens (and it will), you will be under the microscope and everyone will watch how you react. The main thing is that you do react decisively and confidently.

My final parting thought. Hire the best people! If you are the smartest person in the room – you have failed. Be the leader that can orchestrate the best and the brightest and cultivate the team to be as successful as you can. As the "chief" of the security operations, you cannot do it all by yourself and the better you have done to build and nurture your team, the better you can sleep at night. Wishing you the very best!

About the Author

 Bryan Tutor most recently served as Vice President and Chief Information Officer for Elbit Systems of America, LLC, and brings 30 years of experience to the role, providing strategic and technological direction to a $1.3B Business Unit – with focus on enabling business growth, profit enhancement, innovation, and competitive advantage. Bryan also led the integration of a $350M acquisition in 2019.

Since he joined the company in 2016, Bryan's experience leading technically diverse organizations, combined with his unique combination of leadership, process improvement, and operations management capabilities, have allowed him to make significant strides in improving business performance.

Before Elbit Systems of America, Bryan served as CIO for 12-plus years for Triumph Aerostructures/Vought Aircraft where he oversaw enterprise-wide IT strategy and operations, including transformation projects, system deployments for new production sites and leadership through consolidations, relocations, mergers, and acquisitions. His experiences also include P&L Program Leadership, Supply Chain, Engineering, and Strategy Development. During his career, he also worked for Northrop Grumman and LTV Aerospace and Defense in management and engineering positions earlier in his career.

Bryan holds a Bachelors of Science in Mechanical Design Engineering Technology from Oklahoma State University and completed an MBA in IT Management program to further compliment his real-world experience and in-depth skills in business management and strategy.

Additionally, Bryan has earned a Six Sigma Green Belt from the University of Michigan and has attended numerous on-going professional development courses including Global Leadership Summit, Executive Leadership and Finance and Change Management. He is an advisory board member on several local and national level CIO councils and start-up companies.

LinkedIn Profile

Chapter 2.4

THE NEXTGEN CISO

By Sailakshmi Santhanakrishnan (Sai)

NextGen CISO: Adapting to Change that is Constant

Digital Transformation, Evolving Threat Landscape, And Unanticipated Risks Are Leading To The Rise In Nextgen Ciso's

With technological advancements, the organization's operational agility, increasing sophistication in security threats, and unanticipated social and economic crises demand enterprises be flexible and responsive while delivering secure business services. These factors require quick, responsive, and improvised decision-making of the Chief Information Security Officer (CISO) in protecting the enterprise in an increasingly turbulent business, operational, and regulatory environment. A NextGen CISO means that you are an individual who adapts to the agility of the business environment. You influence to bring change to respond to emerging security threats and risks virtually, you

94

are a constant learner of security disciplines, you are a listener, and an approachable leader who can lead the organization in the event of business or security disruption.

About

This chapter outlines the core domains a NextGen CISO can be anticipated to be familiar with, provide expertise on, and consider incorporating into an enterprise's security strategy. Collaborative learning and knowledge exchange among security, risk, and compliance experts with real-world experiences leading global organizations across many industries have provided this chapter's content, aside from the author's involvement in this field as a security, risk, and compliance advisor for global fortune 500 organizations over the last two decades. This chapter will help you focus on critical elements that are required to lead an information security organization in an ever-changing and unpredictable corporate climate.

It will help NextGen CISOs (and those that are exploring the role) to:

- Understand the role

- Elements of Change

- The New Role – As NextGen CISO

- Prepare, Plan, Invest and Recruit - The NextGen Security Professional

Understand the Role

As per Wikipedia's definition:

"A CHIEF INFORMATION SECURITY OFFICER (CISO) IS THE SENIOR-LEVEL EXECUTIVE WITHIN AN ORGANIZATION RESPONSIBLE FOR ESTABLISHING AND MAINTAINING THE ENTERPRISE VISION, STRATEGY, AND PROGRAM TO ENSURE INFORMATION ASSETS AND TECHNOLOGIES ARE ADEQUATELY PROTECTED. THE CISO DIRECTS STAFF IN IDENTIFYING, DEVELOPING, IMPLEMENTING, AND MAINTAINING PROCESSES ACROSS THE ENTERPRISE TO REDUCE INFORMATION AND INFORMATION TECHNOLOGY (IT) RISKS. THEY RESPOND TO INCIDENTS, ESTABLISH APPROPRIATE STANDARDS AND CONTROLS, MANAGE SECURITY TECHNOLOGIES, AND DIRECT THE ESTABLISHMENT AND IMPLEMENTATION OF POLICIES AND PROCEDURES. THE CISO IS ALSO USUALLY RESPONSIBLE FOR INFORMATION-RELATED COMPLIANCE. THE CISO IS ALSO RESPONSIBLE FOR PROTECTING PROPRIETARY INFORMATION AND ASSETS OF THE COMPANY, INCLUDING THE DATA OF CLIENTS AND CONSUMERS."

Although the above definition holds to the core values and responsibilities a CISO has, technology innovation and lucrativeness of the cybercrime market has changed the nature, target, mechanism of security attack, threats, and business outcomes a CISO is expected to protect, defend against, and meet.

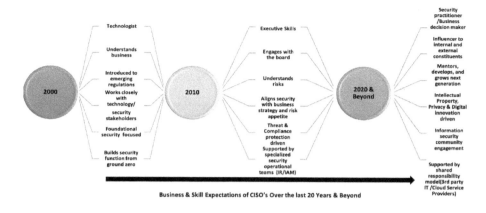

Business & Skill Expectations of CISO's Over the last 20 Years & Beyond

FIGURE 1: CISO'S CHANGING BUSINESS & SKILL
EXPECTATIONS

This is driving the evolution in the role a CISO delivers. Figure 1 illustrates the progression and metamorphosis in the business objectives and desired skills a NextGen CISO is to co-opt. The raising of the bar leads to the NextGen CISO being pursued as a cross-functional business leader, influencer, key ally for new technology adoption, internal and external security advisor, and as a trusted liaison between the risk and audit and business with shared board accountabilities.

Elements of Change

"THE POSITION OF A CHIEF INFORMATION SECURITY OFFICER (CISO) EXISTS AT MANY LARGE FIRMS, BUT IT HAS NOT BEEN A 'C-LEVEL' POSITION. THE CISO WILL HAVE TO BE A POSITION RIGHT UP THERE WITH THE CEO, CFO, AND CIO." - FRED CHON

Elements of change are defined as factors and attributes leading to the drift from the traditional role and responsibilities a CISO holds, to the ones that are anticipated in the future. Critical elements of change, as summarized in figure 2, include:

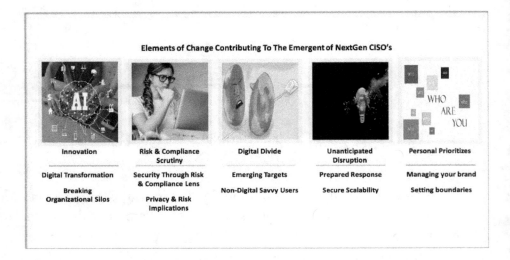

FIGURE 2: ELEMENTS OF CHANGE CONTRIBUTING TO THE EMERGENT OF NEXTGEN CISO'S

- Innovation
- Risk and Compliance Scrutiny
- Digital Divide
- Unanticipated Disruption
- Personal Priorities

INNOVATION

The agility with which business segments are upscaling using digital transformation technologies (i.e., AI, Cloud, IoT,), being modular units, pose new security challenges for the CISO to operate in smaller units embedding security at the grass-root level in a composable enterprise, while ensuring security technology solutions have interoperability amongst the units. This leads to a shift in the NextGen CISO role – one of becoming a key stakeholder in delivering the scaled digitized services, while reporting to the board alongside the business.

RISK & COMPLIANCE SCRUTINY

Frequently evolving threats lead to a growing number of new global regulations (i.e., GDPR). This increases the complexity of implementing the regulatory requirements and defending against multiple international regulators while focusing on preventing breaches and/or avoiding massive financial fines. This paradigm shift calls for CISOs to go from being just a pure technologist, to a risk leader who thinks and articulates security solutions and expenditure in terms of risk, compliance, and privacy.

DIGITAL DIVIDE

Unforeseen circumstances like the pandemic, the strategic embedding of and the growth of smart devices in personal lives, and the incorporation of new technology by corporate elements like Drone and IoT are changing the target and threat landscape from where, how, and through whom the security exploits are triggered. The NextGen CISO requires that they be a connection into the community, so as to raise awareness of these rising vulnerabilities from an unanticipated diverse set of users, from an educator to a local baker, who have been pushed to support remote learning or move to an online business model with minimal or no education on cyber hygiene.

Given the ease of connectivity amongst new technologies, the vulnerability of exploit on the weakest link in the food chain, amongst a digitally divided consumer, a NextGen CISO is now required to broaden the zone of security and anticipate points of security failures occurring from the exploit of an individual to small and large enterprises.

UNANTICIPATED DISRUPTION

In contrast to the digital divide, the corporations are now under pressure to be prepared and scale critical infrastructure to fulfill new business opportunities securely, to align with unpredicted growth patterns, and to adopt emerging technologies, while dealing with nascent digitally security savvy consumers. A NextGen CISO is now expected to be prepared at all times to respond and scale to the digital growth spurts and modernized mechanisms of security attacks. This calls for the NextGen CISO to have a wide range of skills and ability to articulate, influence, negotiate, partner, and draw from a cross-functional set of experts in business, security, risk, compliance, legal, and third party advisory and service providers during the time of a business disruption.

PERSONAL PRIORITIES

It has been observed over the last two decades that the rise in cybercrime, contractual penalties from non-compliance to business customer SLAs, regulatory fines (e.g., GDPR) combined with internal operational and decision-making limitations, and the 'blame culture' in the event of a breach, have created undue physical and emotional pressure on individuals in the CISO role. These aspects are redefining a more collaborative approach to managing and delivering security expectations. These include the NextGen CISO being able to set personal boundaries, delegate, and engage peers in leadership to enable shared decision making, and mentor the next-generation workforce to be guided to assume new roles required for changing times.

The New Role - As the NextGen

"Both the CSO and CISO should have a seat on their company's board," says George Finney, Chief Security Office of Southern Methodist University. "CEOS now get fired because they didn't understand cybersecurity, right? That's a real opportunity for both roles to be there." -Securitymagazine.com

It is essential to observe and accept the contextual variations CISOs are being placed in, requiring changes in their responsibility, demands, skills, and learning. The core characteristics of NextGen CISOs that are needed to bring to this position are:

- **Executive Leadership**

  o Finding their voice at the board: being able to restate security expenditure in terms of business outcomes, risk reduction, and the cost of meeting security and privacy obligations

  o Ability to navigate and be successful across diverse reporting models (i.e., CISO-CIO; CISO-CFO; CISO-CTO; CISO-CRO; CISO-legal Counsel/others), this being a key driver in the ability to spend and obtain more independence, while they chart their path to a successful delivery

- **Personalization**

  o Creating their brand by broadening the zone of influence with both internal and external constituents
  o Use of title (Chief Security Officer vs. Chief Information Security Officer) that equates and connects one as a C-suite

executive allowing independent and influential decision making

- o A champion who builds a security organization based on collaboration, delegation, trust, and empowerment of diverse skills and expertise
- o Effective in dealing with adversity and continuous use of knowledge and skills to showcase the role's significance

- **Preparedness**

  - o Capability to be prepared and respond through small and large-scale disruptions
  - o Be of value and help securely sustain normal operations through accelerated business demands (e.g., enabling remote workforce) in a volatile market climate (e.g., COVID-19)
  - o Drive reprioritization based on risk and business outcomes to address business/technology crisis and failure
  - o Establish a proactive mechanism to be educated on current security trends and demands and transfer them into preparedness and response strategy for the enterprise
  - o Be open and adaptive to new ways of performing the role, such as part-time and virtual CISO.

- **Agility**

  - o Aptitude to adapt and readjust through rapidly changing technology trends
  - o Be an active participant in balancing business vs. security vs. risk
  - o Come anticipating redefinition and new approaches to delivering traditional security (e.g., implementation of segregation of duties through automation)
  - o Focus on inculcating a security culture ground up

      ○   Have a mindset to invest and promote security automation

- **Know Your Space**

      ○   Develop insight into regulatory and privacy commitments
      ○   Be aware of expanding and hybrid (legacy vs. current vs. future technology environments) security landscape
      ○   Determine success criteria for security defense in alignment with business and risk objectives
      ○   Understand your deterrent and threats, reskill, and train to re-strategize defense

Prepare, Plan, Invest & Recruit - The NextGen Security Professional

"CYBERSECURITY TALENT CRUNCH TO CREATE 3.5 MILLION UNFILLED JOBS GLOBALLY BY 2021" -CYBERSECURITYVENTURES.COM

Almost every NextGen CISO is faced with the reality of balancing the deficiency of emerging demand for security professionals against the availability of security talent. Given this, it is critical as the front-runner of a security organization that the NextGen CISO prepares, plans, invests, and recruits creatively. With the proven need for enterprise security, it is time-critical and essential that timely forecasts are in place to leverage and allocate funds to hire the right security personnel.

Decision-makers involved in security hiring should use ingenious approaches to recruitment (e.g., reviewing a strong data analytic candidate for training and hiring for an open threat management role or rehiring part-time organizational retires encouraging lateral moves across functional business segment by non-technical hires). Preparing for the future means investing in the incoming generation through mentorship, internship, and community partnership programs. It also means looking at an untapped and non-conventional pool of security resources like high-schoolers, college freshmen/sophomore candidates, part-time mothers, and/or workforce re-joiners as possible investments into building the security resource pool. Creating a center of excellence and/or resource pipeline using local and regional talent that can remotely support the growing need in security is another outlook NextGen CISO should pursue. Figure 3 provides a holistic approach to preparing, planning, investing, and recruiting the next generation of security talent.

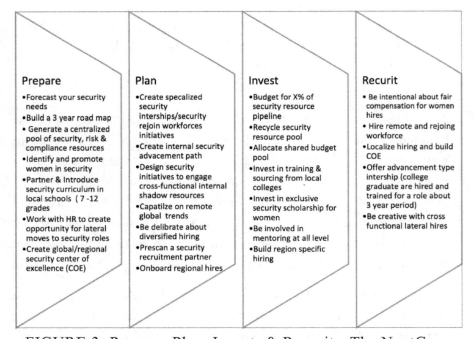

FIGURE 3: Prepare, Plan, Invest, & Recruit - The NextGen Security Professional

While the above factors are essential, it is important that the hiring budgets are secured and utilized to maximize the hire.

Conclusion

The NextGen CISO is viewed as a change agent accepting and acknowledging the digital transformation and adopting the changing demand of their role, services, and organization.

The NextGen CISO is a vital advisor and executor who can influence and bring together the organization to accelerate the business journey securely. NextGen CISOs play a significant role in driving a risk-based approach to security.

All said and done, this role is highly demanding and comes with its own professional pressures, leaving the NextGen CISO to navigate a path that is conducive to an individual's personal needs. The ever-evolving nature of digital transmission and technology enhancements makes the CISO role a moving target, and a NextGen CISO always is a learner, an adaptive leader, creative thinker, and prepared responder.

Research Reference

- https://www.securityforum.org
- https://www.ciosummits.com
- https://securityintelligence.com
- https://www2.deloitte.com/us/en.html
- https://www.bitsecure.co

About the Author

Security, Risk & Compliance Strategist & Advisor and, NextGen Coach

Sai holds Bachelors in Computer Science from India and Masters in CIS with specialization in IT Security from Boston University, USA. Her professional career of 20+ years spans across multiple industries leading and delivering global initiatives for Fortune 100 & 500 companies in IT Security, Risk, Compliance, Privacy & in emerging technologies.

Sai's core strengths are in partnering with the C-suite and business segments to enable their organizations to build IT risk resilience and adoption of cloud strategies while being secure and compliant with global regulations and privacy needs.

Sai has positively influenced the promotion of risk and security awareness programs to improve brand value, Information Protection posture, client trust, and reduction of financial penalties.

Sai is very passionate about enabling youth, women and giving back for social causes. She is the cofounder of 'WeInspire' an organization that mentors the youth of today to be the future leaders, innovators, and creative thinkers.

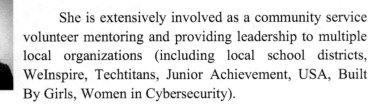

She is extensively involved as a community service volunteer mentoring and providing leadership to multiple local organizations (including local school districts, WeInspire, Techtitans, Junior Achievement, USA, Built By Girls, Women in Cybersecurity).

Believes - " Life is a journey not a destination. Learn from the experiences and relish the path traversed !".

LinkedIn Profile

106

Chapter 2.5

GETTING COMFORTABLE WITH RISK

By Amna Awan

Perspectives - understanding oneself, others, and the organization in roles that require comfort with risk

Lessons learned along my personal journey

Aside from technical knowledge and skills, being a leader in the cybersecurity field, or any field for that matter, requires awareness of self, others, and the organization. It requires taking a step back, seeing the bigger picture, understanding the perspective of others, and ability to balance; it also requires developing a comfort level with living with risk.

Oneself

Careers are journeys, just like life. We can't plan every stop along the way, and we can't predict all the unexpected turns. People who are at senior levels in organizations at times get the question – what path did you take to get to where you are? The implicit assumption in that question is that the person had deliberately charted the course from the start of their working life to the present point. In reality, many unpredictable factors play a part in arriving at the destination.

That is not to say we are completely helpless and should sit back and let luck and chance lead our lives. As the saying goes, luck favors the prepared. There are many common factors that contribute to career and life success that are within one's ability to impact, the first of which is one's personal definition of success.

Generally, within corporate life, having a higher title and salary is considered success. However, each of us needs to evaluate in the context of our own lives, circumstances, and preferences, what success means and not use comparison to others as a marker. The roles we hold within an organization are just that – roles. Each is meant to fulfill an organizational purpose, and each contributes to the overall advancement of the company. Just because one person holds a role equated to the c-suite, while another holds a role equated to junior staff, such is not a reflection on the success of that human being. It is merely a requirement being fulfilled within the organization.

A second factor that is key to one's personal success, whatever that definition happens to be, is the quality of decisions. Almost every moment of our lives is a decision point. Most of these we make out of routine and habit. The smaller routine decisions may seem inconsequential and not warranting our attention. However, it is the cumulative effect of the daily small habits that over time determine our trajectory. Therefore, being mindful and reflective about the small stuff, and course-correcting early and often, helps keep us on a trajectory with a higher likelihood of good outcomes. The bigger decisions that set the more drastic and visible changes in our lives, are the ones we generally give more thought and attention.

The quality of those bigger decisions is not rated by the outcome down the path. There is hindsight involved in looking back and passing judgment. This state involves having information that was not available at the time the choice was made, so it is not a fair assessment. The quality of the decision is based on whether all reasonable information was gathered and evaluated and whether differing perspectives were solicited and considered. Another critical factor in evaluating the quality of the decision, is whether the intention was clear and sincere, and not driven by ego. That is to say, considering the information available, varying perspectives and pros and cons, was the choice made that was the right course of action, as best as could be determined? Or, was it one that focused on what made one look good or feel good in the moment?

A third contributor to one's personal success is having a comfort level with making mistakes. The fear of making errors is related to the worry of how those mistakes will reflect upon oneself. When that trepidation is the driving force behind decisions, the quality of the decision is diminished as thinking is clouded. It is fear and ego that keep us from stretching ourselves at times, and stepping out of our comfort zones, because there lurks the possibility of failure. To grow, however, requires us to step out of our comfort zones and then learn to get comfortable there; and once that space becomes familiar and comfortable, then we step beyond that again. This is a rinse and repeat cycle for growth, which requires facing fear and separating from the thoughts that hold us back in the familiar zone.

Related to that growth cycle, is recognizing and seizing opportunities. Those won't come knocking on our door and present us with a hand calligraphed card that invites us to accept the opportunity. Perhaps on occasion that may happen. Most of the time, however, they will be subtle signs and moments that continually present themselves to those who are paying attention with a clear mind.

A fourth factor to consider is openness to feedback, particularly constructive. The openness is not just the willingness to sit in a performance review meeting and listening to unpleasantries with composure. Rather, it is seeking out critical feedback on work, ideas, and even behaviors, with the intention of learning and improving. It is also being observant of people's remarks and behaviors to glean insights that may be used as feedback. That is a little bit scary and indeed painful at times. However, it is required to understand others' perception of us, so that we may know what to work on for personal improvement. It is uncomfortable to recognize that we have problems; not to just say it casually, but truly accepting that we have areas that need improvement. Yet, it is also wonderful to recognize that we have such problems, as that gives us opportunities to address them and improve. To shut oneself down from acknowledging our issues, is depriving ourselves from ever getting better. It is condemning ourselves to remain in our present state of development forever, which brings to light how important it is to be grateful and mindful of feedback. However, it is essential to not let the feedback be a reflection of our self-worth, and only an opportunity for improvement. It is okay to feel the sting for a little bit, and then have the strength to move past that feeling and figure out a plan to improve. It is not okay to ruminate on the sting, and let it set into fright that keeps us from trying again.

There is one caveat to being open to feedback. There is generally more than one side to every story; however, not all sides are equally valid. Similarly, not all feedback received is equally worthwhile. Before internalizing the feedback, reflect on its source, and the intention. It may be just one data point that is not consistent with other information gathered. We have a choice as to which information to take in and where to initiate action. Just because words are spoken or written, they are not required to be true or believed. It takes a little bit of extra brain energy to use filters to determine validity, and it is energy well spent.

Finally, and perhaps most importantly, it is essential to have a mindset of continuous learning. Comparatively speaking, the pace of change in the world used to be linear, and now in many situations it is exponential. Certainly, that has been the case in the world of technology. To stand still is to fall behind. To keep progressing, we must continue to learn and improve our skills and knowledge.

Others

One observation often presented among junior security professionals is that leadership or other teams don't care about security, or are not doing enough to prioritize the security team's requests. There seems to be an assumption that we, as security professionals, care about the protection of our companies, while others are not concerned about the risks. The reality in most cases is that we as security professionals have not done an adequate job of getting others to understand the presented risk. We live and breathe the threat and vulnerability information on a daily basis; therefore, the concerns are top of mind for us. Those in other functions live a very different reality on a daily basis. The worries that are top of mind for them are ones about which we have very little understanding. We typically don't go out of our way to learn about the priorities of those in finance, marketing, operations, etc. Yet, we feel indignant when not all those functions take security as seriously as we do.

Others outside the security team may not understand and prioritize security concerns, and this is a failure on our part to educate them on the risks. It is not a reflection on their indifference towards the security of the company. In this regard, rather than having a confrontational stance between security and development, or security and operations, some self-reflection is required on the part of security professionals. What are we doing to facilitate understanding, as well as being easy to work with? Security controls are most effective when they are designed to meet the objectives, in a way that is built into the existing processes in a seamless manner with minimal overhead. The challenge to get other teams to improve their security posture becomes a lot easier, as we make doing the right thing, also the easy thing to do. Designing checks that are difficult to implement and creating additional burden on teams, and then expecting those teams to happily comply, is not a recipe for effective risk mitigation. As more companies move to cloud environments and transform technology delivery using agile and DevOps, we, as security professionals, need to focus on reinventing controls that meet the intent. We cannot be slowing down progress by attempting to enforce legacy methods in changing environments.

The Organization

Stepping back and looking at the bigger picture is important, so that we are using our energy and resources effectively. A trap we sometimes fall into is wasting energy in trying to improve things that are already good enough. Consequently, we take away resources from areas that need our attention.

A common example of this is switching to a new security tool for a capability where a good enough product is already in use - a little bit of the shiny object syndrome. We attend security conferences, see vendor demos, or get impressed by the latest analyst report on xyz security product. This technology will be the silver bullet to solve all our security woes so we can sleep better. Instead of seeing reality as it is, we see it as we want it to be. Then we start our pursuit - the meetings, the demos, the assessments, comparisons, procurement, training, calibration, integration, and so on. Where are all these resources invested in the process of getting a slightly better security product coming from? They are coming from the resources that need to be focused on the areas in which gaps exist. And it would be a very rare organization where there are no gaps to address. Is it worthwhile to invest in moving from an A-minus capability to an A capability in one area, when there are other capabilities at D or below in the same environment? The optimization within the silo is at the opportunity cost of the improvement of the whole.

Another perspective to understand in the context of leadership decisions, that at times seem misaligned to our security priorities, is realizing the bigger environment in which we operate. When we see a new zero-day come out, or read about the latest breach, it does feel like the sky is falling. However, from the company leadership perspective, there are other and often bigger risks to consider. In terms of enterprise risk management, cybersecurity is a subset of operational risk. The company also has to manage additional risks including credit, liquidity, market, strategic, compliance, etc. The view from the top is considering all of these additional risks. It makes sense that cybersecurity, while definitely critical to the health and success of an enterprise, is not the only focus of leadership; and that becomes one of the key success factors for cybersecurity leaders – the ability to get other leaders to understand the risk, and prioritize resources to mitigate, when those same resources are to be shared across the organization in addressing multiple other types of risks.

To say that leadership does not care about security is a cop-out for not having articulated the risk effectively to get prioritization. As one moves up in organizations and the scope of responsibility grows, the broader the view becomes into other functions and risks. Effective risk management is key to success - the operative word being 'management' and not elimination. Over time, greater and greater amounts of risks need to be accepted in pursuit of objectives, as long as those risks are managed at acceptable levels. Driving risk lower than those levels takes energy and resources from other necessary pursuits to run and grow the business. Learning to live with and be comfortable with risk is a key quality for progressing within our careers. Not being able to handle that effectively will drive stress to unhealthy levels.

Living with Risk

Whatever one's job and environment, it is fair to say it is accompanied by its own set of challenges and stress. It may also be fair to say that roles in cybersecurity come with a higher level of stress than many other jobs. This is partly due to the nature of the work – protecting the confidentiality, integrity, and availability of the enterprise's resources and data. It is also due to the daily spotlight on the most recent hack, the just identified vulnerability, the latest regulatory action, to name a few factors. Then, there is the daily struggle of knowing what the right thing to do is (from our lens) and convincing others to do that right thing. Others include those holding the corporate purse strings, those in position to make decisions, and each employee with the power to click. It is a daunting task, not only because there are so many complex aspects to most choices, but also because so much of it is beyond our power. That is the part of the stress of our jobs; that is our own contribution – trying to affect things that are beyond our control and getting frustrated in the process.

In that, also lies the key to coping with our stress – the realization that we cannot manage everything. Perhaps those people who may have worn capes in the physical world, and took it upon themselves to right wrongs and save others, are the same kind of people who are drawn to the world of cybersecurity. In the battles in the virtual world, we sometimes feel the weight of the world upon our shoulders. We can understand for example, the nature of vulnerability, and the potential impact of its exploitation. It is clear and obvious to us that something must be done about this, and it must be done now. It is also very frustrating to want others to take that matter as seriously as we do, and we may feel that they don't care, because they are not following our heed. It is very worrying to think about all the potential negative impacts, and in those times, it is important to have the ability to breathe deeply and let it go - let go of the need to control things beyond one's power- and let go of the resistance to what is. That is not to say that we should not be doing our best to identify, assess, and mitigate risks; instead, we should be doing our best every day, and then beyond that, we should not hold on to things we cannot impact. Otherwise, it can easily lead to burning ourselves out.

We cannot achieve perfection in prevention, but we can set high standards and do our best to achieve them, without living in dread of what may happen in the future. When the future becomes the present, then we can do our best in that moment and handle whatever is within our abilities and power. For now, while we plan for the future, we can only live in the present and do our best in this moment, and then just take a deep breath and let go of the rest. Holding on to things we cannot manage takes energy away from things that we can influence. While it may sound frivolous to say let go, it is rather a means to allow ourselves to focus on activities where we can make a difference.

Given we can't achieve perfection in prevention, or even in identification and detection for that matter, a well-prepared response and recovery strategy is critical. A few years ago, we may have recognized the function as incident response and disaster recovery. Today one evolution of those core necessities is broadly resilience, as an intersection of business continuity, cybersecurity, and well-architected technology. Cybersecurity as a stand-alone separate function, or security as an add-on feature, is no longer effective, if it ever was.

Building for resilience requires cyber security professionals, more than ever before, to work collaboratively with other functions, to clearly articulate risk to partners, and to make controls seamless and easy to implement. It also requires us to take a balanced approach to provide broad coverage with appropriate depth vs. having tunnel vision and going deeper in certain areas and missing opportunities to address gaps in other areas.

There are possibly more unknowns than knowns that may ultimately determine the outcome of our efforts. We have to focus on what is within our power to affect, and not get distracted by factors beyond.

About the Author

Amna Awan is an experienced cybersecurity and technology risk leader, with a broad-based professional background. Her entrance into this field was a result of starting Career 2.0. Prior to that, Amna had taken a long career break to focus on her children. During her time away from the outside working world, she obtained her CISSP and developed her skills and knowledge. Thankfully, someone was willing to take a chance on a full-time stay at home mom with a certification and some potential, and so Amna was able to re-enter the workforce and grow in the cybersecurity field.

LinkedIn Profile

Chapter 2.6

CULTIVATING A SECURITY MINDSET

By Anil Varghese

So... do you want to be a CISO?

The role of the CISO is complex, evolving, demands strong mental fortitude, and is in the same vein rewarding, exciting, and continues to be defined as it is a fairly young discipline. At its initial formation the function was primarily seen and regarded as a purely technical focus area, where the tech person was handed over the responsibilities to take on this new task of 'security.' Fast forward 40(+) years, and you'll see the evolution of the information security transition from mainframe, to client/server, to cloud computing. Within that timeframe, the role of the CISO emerged. It is less than thirty years old, being one of the youngest disciplines to hold the C-level title, where Steve Katz is widely recognized as becoming the world's first CISO. I had the opportunity to meet him early in my career, and the fact that remains true is that he has been a consummate business professional, which proved invaluable as he stepped up to respond to the call. Today, the role continues to mature and is viewed as that of a forward-leaning business leader, serving a distinct strategic need across industries, and engaging technology risk executives at the senior leadership teams and Boards.

What capabilities should be brought to bear in cultivating a security mindset? A growth mindset is required and is a shared trait amongst successful CISOs. Loosely, the concept refers to individuals that have a thirst for learning, continuous development, and a willingness to put forth the hard work and determination to succeed. First and foremost, you can transform yourself into becoming a business leader by thinking in terms of the business and bringing your collective years of experience as a risk manager to the table and affording a combined and unique perspective to your organization. Engagement starts as you begin to exercise that muscle regarding business acumen, how you apply security risk management concepts against the backdrop of business priorities and corporate goals. Those that can leverage a differing vantage point to risks, threats, compliance issues, and manifest them into how those matters can or will impact the business or vertical, are highly regarded, provided the organization is ready and positioned to engage in those terms.

Years ago, one of my early managers coined the phrase, 'Hacking r00t is a state of mind' as the hidden message for a 'capture the flag (CTF) exercise,' which was a part of capstone penetration testing course. I took that message to heart in identifying and viewing probable risks to the environment and defining measures to mitigate those threats. By way of illustration, when the Apple iPod was first introduced to the market, I saw this as a data exfiltration tool and possible threat vector; we subsequently started planning our approach, which led to port lockdown policies, restrictions, and technical safeguards being deployed. That encompasses the mentality and distinct mindset that is essential to how you approach greenfield challenges and can serve in building a foundational baseline in thinking and acting securely.

The beauty of the function and discipline is that its domains are still being discovered; just as the field of medicine is vast, wide, and consists of areas of specialization, so too is our field of practice. Today's hot skills revolve around scripting/coding, cloud, and understanding AI/ML precepts; tomorrow it will evolve into quantum computing and its impacts to secure ecosystems downstream, while raising societal and ethical implications. Per the same, leaders who can engage in the technical aspects of these emerging technologies, also grasping the overarching effects and downstream impacts, provide their firms a stronger footing. Having a strong grasp of the technical subject matter is a prerequisite at this level, the application of complex risk management principles as it pertains to the business, is that which is sought after.

ENGAGING THE BUSINESS AND THE BOARD

How do you engage?

It's all about establishing key relationships at the onset - at this level of leadership, establishing key relationships is critical not only to your own success, but to the success of the initiatives and programs you put forth. What worked elsewhere may not work in your current situation – this where you should pull upon those collective experiences and bring those insights to the table.

- **Look, Listen, and Learn**
- **Learn the Business**

  - It is not about you, it's about the business
  - What is the organization's corporate strategy?

o   Know the financials, dive into the industry, immerse yourself, and gain knowledge of the space in which you now operate

- **Understand the executive leadership team and Board make-up**
- **Develop keen relationship management skills - relationships matter!**

The initial demands of the role were those of engaging as an operational technical security architect and regulatory compliance guru. Now, the CISO role is constantly evolving and will continue doing so as the discipline matures. The role today requires leaders in mature organizations to serve as trusted advisors and strategists that can not only adapt to changes in the threat landscape, but can also provide a balanced opinion on technology risks posed to the organization.

Look, Listen, and Learn: What is in place? How did the organization get here? Assess the current state, not just from a security posture, but also from the business perspective to garner insights. Get your hands on all relevant financial reports that paint a picture of the past, current, and proposed/planned state of the business. Read industry analysis pertaining to your sector and those that you rely on from a third-party standpoint. Understand and learn risk management principles, to be astute in providing options and alternatives to the risk(s) the firm is entertaining. As an example, more and more we rely on third parties, which has become more pervasive due to the volume and type of data breaches, and something necessary due to the competitive advantage they give, along with best-of-breed capabilities afforded to us through these partner services (HR/Payroll/outsourced application development/security and audit services). This illuminates your understanding of what additional focus areas require thought, as you begin to devise the foundation for your short-term tactical and long-term strategic plans/roadmaps.

We serve the business… not the other way around. Information security (or assurance) outside of the Department of Defense affiliated apparatus and intel community (IC), must be carved out to meet the needs of the business. Security in this context for most businesses is a balancing act, as the strategies and measures employed cannot impede productivity or otherwise impact the firm's ability to be agile in the face of market competitors. Take in point the current pandemic. CISOs overnight had to grapple with what controls were under consideration to be dialed back and which ones were heightened per a user community that was now 100% remote, to ensure their respective employee base was both operational as well as secure.

The CISO mission is to provide the means to propel the business forward through a creative and dynamic security-conscious approach. More so, it is to enable leadership to make qualified risk-based decisions, with timely insights against perceived threats, and with the flexibility and responsiveness to meet fluctuating market conditions.

Trusted Advisor and Strategist

'Trusted Advisor' is a status earned by those leaders who can sell security across the organization, are perceived by the business as a risk manager, and serve as the go-to resource in solving problems – a business enabler. The 'Strategist' serves and pulls together connective threads, creating a tapestry that is summed up as roadmap and vision that aligns squarely with corporate business objectives. As a strategist, you may also be called upon to challenge the status quo to drive alignment, transformation, and to demonstrate value in planned investments.

• The role also requires the CISO to wear the hat of Influencer and Negotiator

• Influencer – CISOs only have a limited amount of authority, and as an influencer, you must gain the respect, trust, and expertise of your team, peers, and leaders in how you go about engaging others. Whether that's operational strategy on deploying patches, engaging in delicate conversations on ownership and responsible parties that should be part of the solution, the role of influencer plays a key role. Finding balance is critical in achieving your objectives, while enabling the business to be agile without forgoing security risk management tenets. CISOs do not have carte blanche authority to decree the rule of law; they must operate within structural constructs and accepted cultural norms of the firm. Seasoned leaders must be comfortable in exercising their sphere of influence as part of their duties to execute initiatives. This capacity empowers leaders to build credibility and legitimacy amongst their peer groups and leadership alike.

• Negotiator – Security, outside of a direct violation of corporate policy is matter of give and take. Successful leaders are able to engage their peers, business units, executive leaders, and the Board. Being able to walk in another's shoes not only provides perspective, but also garners empathy, when applied correctly. There is a constant ebb and flow between executive staff and business leaders on what makes it to the docket as strategic priorities. In the end, you are charged with raising risk to leadership to allow them to make the right call. That call, to accept or negate risk, ultimately resides with them, but how you deliver that message could be decisive in that process.

- We are selling trust, whether it is to internal stakeholders or external customers.

The Great Communicator

Communication skills are paramount at this level of engagement, whether written or verbal - how you convey ideas, approaches, risks, facts, and informed opinions, actually matter. As your constituency continues to grow and become more inclusive of your program(s), plans, and overarching enterprise strategies, the capacity to tailor and customize the message to those varying audiences is paramount. The CISO must craft their message to meet their audiences (staff/leaders/Board/customers/stockholders) wherever they sit within the corporate structure. Being able to simplify security and risk-related topics to both technical and non-technical audiences is critical to success and getting necessary stakeholder buy-in.

Key Tenets for any CISO

- Relationship management skills are paramount; relationships truly matter

    o It's equally important to not come across as disingenuous, as people can sense this quickly. If this skill set does not come across naturally, then it becomes for you an area where improvement and growth are needed.

- Technical prowess at this level are table stakes - new technologies/concepts are expected to be learned.
- Understanding cultural dynamics and norms are crucial to deciphering what mechanisms you can employ to engage each of your stakeholders.

- You must undertake the role of 'the influencer.' Success will be measured by those that are adept in working across the aisle
- You must be adaptable, calm under pressure, and develop the wherewithal to make decisions without all the facts or information at your disposal.
- You must be strategic in your endeavors in maturing any technology risk management program.
- If you do not see yourself as a business leader and carry yourself as one, then no one else will.
- Security at this level is a people business. Yes, technology is leveraged, but it is only part of the equation in solving business risk issues.
- What approaches can I employ to be better equipped?

  - Learn the business, become a student of the industry vertical you are a part of
  - Seek out perspective, whether that's in your current or future roles; roles permitting s you to become a better operator and leader
    - Why do great business leaders, recommend or prescribe to leadership books? They have a growth mindset and want to leverage learnings from battle tested peers.
      - Get on those reading list(s), review case studies and lessons learned
      - Think globally, gain current perspective. Read what the business reads.
        - (e.g. WSJ, Financial Times (FT), The Economist, /Fortune…)
    - Find a mentor, to show you the ropes and offer constructive external viewpoints.
    - Get an ally on the Board, to be your champion and navigate engagement process.

- The learning never stops! All leaders position themselves as lifelong students.
- Every crisis is an opportunity (from pandemics to breaches, to changes in the regulatory and compliance landscape).

   o These scenarios provide an opportunity to reset, reflect, or provide a vehicle to push through other tangible efforts that will ultimately strengthen the posture of your programs.
   o They also provide a new engagement channel for messaging that may have been unavailable before.

- Seek out perspective, whether that's in your current or future roles, or industry trends; this is what permits you to become a better operator and leader.
- Pay it forward and become mentor to others.
- All firms are not created alike; it's imperative to understand corporate dynamics **(mission/goals/vision/roadmap/culture nuances).**

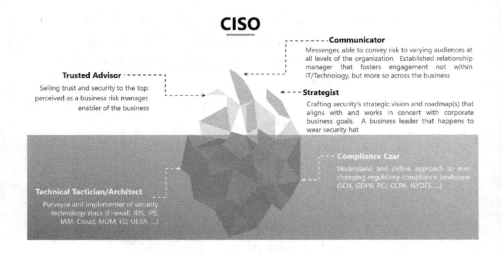

My Personal Journey

My interest in security began at an early age back in 1988 with the outbreak of the Robert Morris worm, and getting my first glimpse of this field. I began researching the field of information assurance (IA) or information security (INFOSEC), which at that time existed predominantly only within the military and intelligence agency realms. Subsequently, I became immersed in many facets of this nuanced space, as it was just entering into the public/private sectors. I was eager to seek out opportunities that were varied and would lend themselves to providing global perspectives. So began my career in the consulting arena with the Big 6/Big 4 at the time, which laid the groundwork for other consulting opportunities and my own practice. Being in that arena for over a decade allowed me to see how other businesses and industries operated. Consulting provides indoctrination into firefighting – a skill and trait that becomes obligatory, as it provided first-hand knowledge of the time-sensitive issues those industry verticals (financial services, manufacturing, technology, pharma/healthcare, etc.) were facing head-on and how best to tackle them, while bringing the most complimentary solutions to the forefront. This also provided a vehicle to be exposed to multiple industries, some of which I enjoyed and thrived in, some that I didn't.

I have been fortunate, lucky, and privileged enough to serve as a five-time CISO (one in an acting capacity), across a few different business verticals. In that time, during the past fifteen years, and through that lens, I have seen a multitude of ups and downs across the industry, witnessed times of economic hardship, experienced firsthand firms downsizing or undergoing restructures, and have been engaged in M&As. There is never a dull moment within our chosen field. You must learn to adapt to an ever-changing environment and prevailing market conditions that may affect your industry. Just as the threat landscape changes daily, if not hourly, so too does the capacity to embrace change, ambiguity, risk, and seizing on those opportunities in being decisive in trying to make the right call.

Final Takeaways

The great thing about security is that it permeates throughout our everyday lives, so what we do in the office impacts our teammates and their families when we leave the office or log-off. These days there is no respite from connectedness. No one gets disconnected when we 'leave the office,' they merely engage our connected world through a different medium, be that mobile phone, tablet, smart watch, IoT, or smart appliances. We are all still plugged in and have to stay cognizant of and ensure our teams are vigilant in acting securely. I typically end our newsletters with 'Stay Vigilant & Stay Secure;' it's a mantra I hope conveys the importance of what we do and the exciting opportunities in front of us as a profession.

- Pursue your passions, even if the road isn't paved yet – so you get to define it!
- The profession is highly collaborative; with like-minded passionate leaders who are trying to mature the collective.
- For current and future CISOs, get plugged into the community and help define what the profession becomes.

Anil Varghese, a renowned industry veteran with over two decades of global experience in the information security and risk management arena – including stints at American Express and Sony Electronics, Inc. – currently serves as Senior Vice President and Chief Information Security Officer (SVP/CISO) within the financial services industry. In his most recent management roles, he has been charged with technology governance and maturing assurance programs at Blackstone portfolio companies.

Under his leadership, Anil had direct responsibility for setting strategic direction on IT risk, security, compliance, and privacy issues. He has been engaged to support sensitive M&A due diligence initiatives and fostered key strategic relationships with a keen eye towards the needs of the business. He has established credibility across corporate boardrooms by focusing on managing risk and not promoting fear. Anil also served as an esteemed thought leader and security evangelist across the industry for PayPal and others.

Anil serves as a go-to advisor for Fortune 500 firms and startup clients alike on IT risk management matters and is a sitting Board member at Southern Methodist University (SMU) in developing their master's and undergrad cyber program(s). He also provides guidance in a security and privacy thought leadership capacity bringing unique insights to investors that aim to bring innovative solutions to the marketplace by engaging with numerous private equity (PE) and venture capital (VC) firms alike (Greylock, Work-Bench, LightSpeed, Landmark, etc.). Anil recently completed the Global Policy in Cybersecurity program at Harvard University's Kennedy School of Government. He is an active member of the information security/assurance community, including roles as a presenter/speaker to ISSA, Blackhat, CISO Roundtable, InfraGard, ISACA, and the FBI.

LinkedIn Profile

Chapter 2.7

WHAT IS YOUR 3-LEGGED STOOL?

By Wayne Self

In 2003, I was the Network and Security Manager for a small startup company in the Midwest. My accountability was for all the IT Operations, except for the development teams. I was informed by the CEO at my time of hire that the strategic objective of the organization was to grow itself exponentially and then sell or complete an IPO within 24 months; we were Venture Capital owned and their interest was a return on their investment.

Working for a startup has many positives and negatives, which I could talk about for days, but I will leave that to another time. At that point in my career, the positives outweighed the negatives in every way, so I accepted the role. That role has been the most rewarding of my 20+ years in Information Technology and it increased my understanding of business operations in ways I would never have thought.

In late 2005, the company sale was announced, and we were sold to a global organization in the Northeast. That organization had its own datacenters, so we were asked to relocate our Disaster Recovery site and "flip the switch" to migrate the operations there.

The ability to do this with no downtime was vital to the Technology Services Agreement (TSA).

It was during my time in the Northeast that I received an especially important lesson in communicating with executives. The kickoff meeting was held in a conference room that was larger than any one I had been in, so it was a bit overwhelming. The room, combined with the view of Lower Manhattan out of the windows, left me a bit starstruck.

As the people gathered in the room for the migration kickoff, we were joined by a few of the acquiring company's senior executives. The meeting started with one of the executives asking me who I was and what my role was in the TSA efforts. I stammered for about two minutes of what I remember being gibberish, so I finally just stopped talking. I was shaken up a bit and this feeling stayed with me the entire meeting.

Once the meeting ended, I joined my facility escort who made a comment that went something like "Well, that wasn't very smooth, but you are a technical person so not much was expected, I guess. You definitely have to get your elevator speech prepared." I had never heard of an elevator speech, so I researched the definition, and I knew exactly what he was telling me.

I thought about my elevator speech over the next 6 months as my role ended after the migration was complete. I needed something I could say in any pressurized situation and it needed to be delivered without hesitation and in a well thought out manner. This is when I came up with my 3-Legged Stool speech.

What is a 3-Legged Stool you ask? If you have a stool that you sit on and it consists of one or two legs, it requires you to lean on one direction or another and it never really balances without effort. In short, a 3-Legged Stool provides balance, and all three legs balancing equally is the objective. I have had a three-legged stool for all my roles, but I will speak to the ones I have used in the manager and executive roles. These roles are very different roles with different objectives.

MY MANAGER LEVEL 3-LEGGED STOOL

My Manager's 3-Legged Stool consists of three legs that I can speak to at the drop of a hat:

- Stability
- Maturity
- Security

STABILITY

The first leg I will cover is "Stability." This should be a foundational trait for all IT departments. Without stability, we are not the partner we need to be in support of the business. Always remember that IT can be considered an "expense" or an "enabler" and we always should desire to be an enabler.

My lesson in instability came from working with an IT department that had a very immature policy and process status. Policy and process ensure there is a commonality of how a department operates; it is the shared morays of the teams. The development team would deploy updated code without consideration for a change control process. When the code was ready to deploy, the administrative staff would update the system, thus knocking customers offline and the calls to the Helpdesk would start to roll in.

This lack of a consistent process based on the policy and best practices for code deployment had a measurable cost of more than $100,000 an hour in lost revenue and reputational loss with our customers. This bad practice does not move us toward being an enabler, and soon we would be viewed as a cost center. This issue was addressed by the introduction of our second leg, Maturity.

MATURITY

The second leg is Maturity. As a result of the first leg being tremendously wobbly, we hired a new CIO who brought experience with mature and much larger organizations. His first step was to stop all code deployments into the production system that did not have his approval. His second step was to create System and Network Diagrams so we ensured we understood connectivity and data flows, which would eventually strengthen the understanding of our deployments. While this sounds quite drastic, he was buying time to create policy and process to ensure there were peer reviews from the coding teams and that the administration teams were not deploying the code changes without getting an approval process.

This change was the initial check and balance of the team's processes and it was based on a solid, proven policy framework. We went on to implement Change Control, Code Release, Segmented Environments, Architecture Diagrams, and many more useful tools that we could refer to when making decisions. This brought the maturity required to provide the stability to the organization we needed. Our downtime was reduced, we passed critical audits that led us to bigger clients, and reached the objective of selling the company. We were now able to address the final leg of the stool, which is… Security.

SECURITY

The final leg of the 3-Legged Stool is Security. If you are working in an environment where there is no stability and no maturity, you will not be able to create the balancing leg of Security. While security has always been important, it is now considered vital to organizations. This is one reason there are dedicated Security Teams, Chief Information Security Officers, Security Analysts, and other dedicated roles aligned with protecting company assets.

If you think back to the issues of instability I mentioned earlier, where untested code changes happened at any time, you will see how difficult it would be to make sure there are security checks and balances in place; you would almost have to set up defenses to alert to just the changes themselves! It is exceedingly difficult to secure something that is undocumented and always changing at random intervals. It is particularly important that security become part of the conversation long before the changes occur. This is one of the main themes in DevSecOps, which will have to be covered at another time.

I have attempted to always use a wobbly security leg to strengthen the maturity leg. It is wise for a Security Manager to align with a security framework (CyberSecurity Framework, NIST Series, OWASP, ISO 270001, etc.) even if there is no mandate to do so. This thought goes all the way back to "if you can't measure it, you can't manage it" which should result in a gap document that drives the strengthening of all 3 legs at the same time. I will leave this thought with you, "compliance can only help security, but security can deliver compliance."

MY EXECUTIVE LEVEL 3-LEGGED STOOL

When you reach the executive level of an organization, you have to shift your attention to working directly with your business partners to promote your team as the business enabler I spoke of earlier. Your Directors/Managers, hopefully, will be utilizing the Stability, Maturity, and Security legs, which leaves you to start using your new 3-Legged Stool that aligns your team with your organizational objectives.

My Executive Level 3-Legged Stool consists of these three legs that I can speak to at the drop of a hat:

- Time
- Talent
- Treasure

TIME

The first leg of my Executive 3-Legged Stool is Time. Time is something that is limited in nature and is a resource you must manage closely for your department to be successful. You must treat your resources' time as if it is a bank account, in that you only have so much time to spend before there are penalties due to a negative balance. I have worked for several organizations where time is treated as an unlimited resource. By this, I mean that any project that our business partners expect IT to deliver are added to a queue of project deliverables and prioritized for action, sometimes by who made the request. Your role as the CISO is to ensure that there is always time in the bank to deliver projects based on your team's availability.

Your goals should be to keep a ledger of time for your team's resource availability. If you think of this in the most common of terms, each of your teammates' annual time availability is 2,000 hours at the beginning of every year and every project will pull hours from that bank.

TALENT

The second leg of my Executive 3-Legged Stool is Talent. Now that you understand the banking analogy, you will need to repeat it for the skillset of each person on your team. As an example, a Security Analyst has 2,000 hours to provide to the ledger every year. A Project Manager may have the full 2,000 hours available so their availability may overshadow the other banks on the team. They will need to remove "keeping the lights on" time from their bank based on their role; the remaining hours are their project availability. You repeat this process for each of your teammate's skills to provide a solid matrix and ledger. This exercise should be completed at the beginning of each project year so you can calculate team-tasking availability.

Now that you have hours of availability, you need to plan for the level of talent you need on each project. Different security analysts have differing levels of skills. This must be taken into consideration for your projects to deliver successfully. One security analyst may only take ten hours to complete a task where another may take thirty, so you always need to adjust the ledger based on project needs. You can substitute one for the other but there may be a time penalty on the ledger.

Use your ledger to update your peers on the time and resource needs of the organization to deliver their expected projects. This engagement ensures you are delivering the services to the business that they find most important for their needs. I will have more to say about this below.

TREASURE

Earlier, I mentioned IT as being an "expense" or an "enabler." While we should always strive to be a business enabler, some of your peers will be solely interested in the expenses of the project. This is quite normal, so it is vital that you be able to speak about the financial ratios associated with the project such as return on investment, return on capital, and capital expense vs. operational expense. Each company treats the importance of these terms with a different preference, so use your time with the Chief Financial Officer to uncover their preferred terms to use.

It is the treasure that often determines which of the company projects is the priority. It is important to remember that the security projects you are driving are only a small part of a larger portfolio of projects across the organization, so you have to be able to support the needed justification for your projects. There may be years where you have minimal project approvals, so during those times I have always found it best to help your peers on their projects to see business processes where security could be automated with systems you already have in-house.

You may be wondering how these three legs work in concert? By keeping a ledger of the hours of team availability, you can determine if you have enough staffing to complete the projects your business partners are requesting. If you do not have the hours in your ledger of resources, you have a few choices. You can hire more people to deliver the projects, and using your ledger to do so tells you exactly the talent you need. You can decide to contract with a staffing firm to onboard temporary staffing until your project delivers. This also often allows you to onboard talent you cannot afford on a full-time basis, which also has an added benefit for your current team in learning new skills. The company "treasure" will drive what your best options are, which is why you should always update the leadership team on points of failure in resources.

These three legs must always be at front of mind when you are approached by your peers for new projects. I have never been a

"NO" person with my first answer to a project request. I prefer to give the requester options such as...

Yes, we can do that (my ledger has the room!)

Yes, we can do that (but I will need to hire another Security Analyst or bring on a contractor to do so)

Yes, we can do that (could you please help me prioritize this need into our company project portfolio so we can see if something needs to fall off the schedule?)

I have provided options for them and at the same time where needed, and I have asked them to help me with any conversations on priorities to the other executives. Most often, if you have your ledger ready, your resources of availability and the treasure associated with the cost of the new project, you will arrive at the best solution for the organization.

About the Author

 Wayne Self is an IT Operations and CyberSecurity leader with a proven record of quantifying and mitigating business risk. He has twenty years of execution across industries that include SmartGrid, Financial, Insurance, Healthcare, Retail, DoD, and Aviation.

Wayne has most recently been accountable for global security operations across the U.S., UK, Ireland, France, Singapore, Australia, Romania, and Canada. At those sites, he directed the security and compliance engagements aligned with being a Prime Contractor and a subcontractor for the largest commercial and military organizations across the globe.

Wayne has implemented controls supporting various regulatory frameworks since 2005, which included the education the organization of the requirements and benefits of each. The frameworks have included PCI-

DSS, SSAE16-SOCII, HIPAA, NIST, and the most recent CyberSecurity Maturity Model Certification (CMMC). In 2012, as the Information Security Officer for Aclara Technologies, he guided the successful "pass" on an initial attempt for the SSAE16-SOCII audit for our software as a service organization. This resulted in the SmartGrid business selling into larger markets and reducing future RFP processing times by more than 50%. He is currently implementing the CyberSecurity Maturity Certification for a global aviation company in support of their global defense contracts in support of the U.S. DoD.

Wayne holds a Masters of Business Administration from Webster University and a bachelor's degree in Computer Science from St. Martins University. He is active in the CyberSecurity Collaboration Forum for CISOs and is an active member in the Alamo ISC2 community. Wayne holds multiple cybersecurity certifications.

- Computer Information System Security Professional (CISSP)
- Certified Chief Information Security Officer (C|CISO)
- Certified Ethical Hacker (CEH)
- Information Technology Infrastructure Library (ITIL)
- Certified USAF Air Traffic Controller (USAFATC)

LinkedIn Profile

Chapter 3.1

COLLABORATION AS A CYBER SECURITY STRATEGY

By Jorge Mario Ochoa

C urrently, about 70% of my teachers are Millennials and about 10% are Centennials. I have had the opportunity to learn from great professionals—Generation X and Baby Boomers—who have added a lot to the advancement of my career. The only constant thing is change, and I have learned that I must unlearn, that is, forget what I have already learned, so as not to have prejudices that limit me to learning new ways to find solutions. I have learned to listen more and talk less, to surround myself with new generations who have different visions and strategies. I really like that quote from the Dalai Lama that says, "When you talk, you just repeat something you already know. But when you listen, you might learn something new."

As Albert Einstein said, "The measure of intelligence is the ability to change." In the following lines, I would like to share some of my mistakes, lessons learned, and insights to today's leaders who are confronting issues and challenges faced by cybersecurity professionals.

In school, I never liked history. From a young age, I had to study and memorize everything without the teacher explaining why, and even more importantly, for what. In college, I had amazing professors who taught me in such a way that I am now passionate about history. Those professors taught me that history allows us to understand which strategies were successful, what strategies failed, and what we can learn so as not to make the same mistakes again. When we are passionate about what we do and are interested in people, we can transcend the present state, as I am doing now, sharing my professors' works and thoughts with my family, friends, and now to you, positively affecting many lives.

At the moment I am writing this text, we find ourselves in a pandemic that has radically changed the way we work and live. This pandemic showed us that it is possible to change quickly and that we can adapt to change. It also showed us that many organizations were not prepared with a business continuity plan. On paper, they had business continuity plans for fire, earthquake, flooding, etc. but not for the unknown, like a pandemic.

A hundred years ago, we had a plague. There were many lessons to be learned, processes to be improved, people to be trained, etc. We had a hundred years to prepare, but we did not, or we did, but it was not enough. A business continuity plan includes three basic pillars—People, Processes, and Technology. If there is an earthquake, we need people to be able to continue operating from their homes or alternate sites. For this, they need basic tools, such as a computer and connectivity, processes that tell us what we need to do, and people trained to manage the crisis. It has been more than obvious that many organizations did not have something as basic as a VPN or a laptop. Many organizations only had desktop computers and had never done tests to work remotely. More importantly, many organizations were reluctant to work remotely and did micro-management, because they were too afraid to trust people.

Statistics have usually been used, in many cases, just to communicate what happened or what mistakes were made, but very rarely to shape the future. Every day we see statistics, but very rarely do we see statistics being evaluated, and action plans based on it being formulated for the future. Cybersecurity threats will always be much greater than the resources to deal with those threats. It is so important to look at the big picture and have a team to help carry out the strategy. Each department has its own objectives, and understanding the objectives of other departments will allow us to identify common goals to achieve—the goals of the organization, not just the specific goals of our department.

When I was young, I had the opportunity to study computer science. I was about 14 years old when I started studying DOS (Disk Operating System). I know, you have figured out my age. However, if you also remember DOS, you are probably losing hair too. I started studying computer science at the suggestion of my uncle who has always been a fundamental pillar in my professional career. He is the kind of mentor who actually brings out the best in you.

When I was 17, I bought my first computer. After saving for many months, I was finally able to buy my computer with my salary and it was extremely rewarding. A few days later, I bought a computer maintenance and repair book that was on sale. I liked it so much that I then signed up for a computer maintenance and repair course. Months later, still 17, I was hired to repair computers and do electrical installations. It was the 90s and, at that time, being able to assemble clones and clean computers made you an "Expert." I was fortunate to have a co-worker who did not question my knowledge and experience (which, to be honest, was just level 1 on a scale of 1 to 10). He taught me everything he knew. While he was in charge of repairing the computers, I was in charge of the electrical installations, since I studied electronics at school. I will not lie to you; I caused a couple of short circuits, but no fire, luckily. I greatly appreciate my partner's patience explaining to me and sharing all his knowledge without prejudice or selfishness. Most professionals are not like him; they use something called "professional zeal" and say, "It took me 2 or 3 years to learn, so you should learn by yourself." Fortunately, that did not happen to me at that stage of my career.

A few months passed and I saw an ad looking for a teacher in computer maintenance and repair. Fat chance—I was just 17 and never taught before. However, I have always believed that the worst thing that can happen to one is to be told "No you can't do it." Prior to the interview, I read and re-read that computer maintenance and repair book I purchased with which I started my professional career. When I showed up for the interview, there was the owner of the company. He conducted the interview without pre-judging me. He was looking for a teacher and had a list of typical interview questions. His business was new and he not only needed a teacher, but also someone to help him start his business from scratch.

After answering routine questions, I took the initiative to tell him that I even had a course structure, and a reference book, and that my vision was that the course should be 100% practical and that for this we could buy broken computers at very low cost for the first practical classes, to avoid damaging new computers. The business owner was so impressed that he took the risk and hired me with the condition of getting me on a payroll if the students' evaluations turned positive.

Before each class, I prepared my content exhaustively. I did not want to be asked questions that I would not be able to answer. This experience taught me that when we do not judge people by their experience or titles, we could get to know more about them;

and if we give them the opportunity, this can generate an even greater commitment from them. It also taught me that you learn a lot more when you teach than when you are a student. At the age of 18, I started my first company. Even if it did not turn out to be successful, it rendered me many lessons that I still appreciate to this day.

Over a year later, I saw an opportunity at the United Nations. By then I was about 19 years old. Again, my chances of getting that job were extremely low, yet, I made it. It was a different world. For me it was advanced technology and systems. That was the first time I met Novell Networks. I learned a lot. It was a real challenge, but dedication and persistence allowed me to learn quickly, to the point that in a few weeks, I was already the person in charge to fix the most complicated cases. I then realized that sharing knowledge, apart from being the right thing to do and it being about personal satisfaction, also allowed me not to overload myself with work and be a bottleneck in the process. It is better to have team players who share knowledge instead of lonely players.

After a few years, I decided to return to my dream of being an entrepreneur. Like many businessmen, I dedicated all my time and effort to my company. For some time, the company did very well but ultimately it failed to achieve my expected results. However, the experience made me reflect and made me realize that for those years that I had dedicated all my time and energy to my company, my relationship with my family and friends fell by the wayside. However, my family and friends have always supported me. It was the best opportunity to reflect, to realize that on many occasions I was a boss, but not a leader. I was so focused on the results that I forgot that my results were interdependent, that my goals were not impacted only by my work but also by the work of my team, and vice versa. In college, I attended many subjects—math, statistics, physics, etc. However, I wasn't taught how to be a leader or how to develop a team.

It is up to us to see our experiences as opportunities or failures. After closing the company, I had to look for work and it was not an easy task. However, that experience made me humbler and it made me value my family and friends much more. But what do all these have to do with cybersecurity? You'll see it in a few more paragraphs.

For several months of looking for work, I identified patterns in job offers. There was a high demand for IT professionals; however, there was also a high supply of IT professionals. But there was an area that had very little demand and also very little supply for - it was cybersecurity - and at that time, I realized that this was the future and I had no training in cybersecurity. I realized that to be able to qualify for a cybersecurity position I have to be knowledgeable of the standards and frameworks of COBIT, ISIL, and 27001. I looked for no-cost courses that came with certifications, studied hard, got my certificates, and started applying for cybersecurity positions. The strategy worked and I got my chance. My first challenge was to change the perception of cybersecurity and auditing, then seen as "stoppers" or the "No, you can't do this or that" department.

From the story we were told about Adam and Eve in paradise, it seems that throughout human evolution, the forbidden has always been very attractive. (In fact, I think Apple is so popular due to its logo. "The Bitten Apple… I forbid this fruit."). Several years ago, in Guatemala, smoking in public places became forbidden. It was believed that the negative impact of this on the tobacco industry would be very high; instead, tobacco sales increased dramatically.

It is not the same to say, "DO NOT use the same password for your personal and corporate accounts." To say, "Remember to use different passwords for your personal and corporate accounts to protect yourself." The "What" is important but the "Why" is even more important. Today, a meme could achieve better results than an 80-slides presentation. You must have seen Simon Sinek's Gold Circle Speech about the "What," "How," and "Why"—the "Why" is much more important than the "What" and that is why Apple is #1 globally - because it started with the "Why."

One of the biggest challenges for a CISO is how to create a security culture. I understand that I am not an expert in human resources, leadership, internal communication, marketing, etc. and that an awareness campaign can have excellent content, but if it fails to be understood and connect with the audience, then it cannot be successful. We need to understand the goals of other departments, in order to find out how our own goals could be aligned, so that we all collaborate and work as only one team.

For several months, I worked in conjunction with human resources, internal communication, marketing, and other areas that played an important role in implementing **OUR** program to promote a security culture. "Our" is in bold because it has a totally changed meaning. I went from an independent approach to an interdependent approach, where we all bring value and all fight as one team, a winning team.

Collaboration as Cybersecurity Strategy was so successful that it served as the basis for creating https://cyberheroes.app/ an Information Security Awareness training based in gamification, and in 2017, I was awarded by (ISC)2 as the Senior Information Security Professional of America and also by the EC Council for the most innovative Cybersecurity Project Globally at the Global CISO Forum.

Collaborative work let me know why some strategies we had implemented had not been successful. Something as basic as knowing that the organization where we implemented this strategy happened to have more than 70% Millennials and 5% Centennials. That small detail, which I was not aware of or did not understand at the time, totally changed the strategy.

Several years ago, Colgate toothpaste launched an extraordinarily successful campaign. It was a remarkably simple campaign, which consisted of edited photographs showing people who had six fingers or did not have one ear but had dirty teeth. The first thing people who looked at those photographs noticed were the stains on their teeth. It was an amazingly simple but incredibly successful campaign because it showed how important it is to have clean teeth (obviously, using their toothpaste).

I did not know much about customer experience, internal communication, or marketing, so having the best of all teams and working on a common goal allowed us to design an entire experience around the security culture program. I was finally thinking outside the box and since 2016, I have had the opportunity to speak in America, Europe, and Asia in the field of NeuroHacking, which is focused on disruptive thinking in Cybersecurity. In 2020, working in collaboration, I had the opportunity to launch the first NeuroHacking.net conference with assistance from more than 21 countries.

The more you share, the more you learn. I wanted to write a book in 2020, but I was not able to. Then, I met Paola Saibene, who introduced me to Abu Sadeq, a humble leader who invited me to collaborate on his book. The funny thing is that I met Paola, because several months ago I talked about cyberbullying in a webinar organized by (ISC)2 Guatemala Chapter, the chapter that I lead, and my compatriot María Scarmardo saw my presentation. Then she introduced me to Paola to collaborate with. I am so grateful with María, Paola, and Abu for this opportunity.

There is a success case that I really like - the Pet Rock case. In April 1975, Dahl was in a bar (which is now the tasting hall of the Beauregard vineyards in Bonny Doon), listening to his friend's complaints about his pets and this gave him the idea for the 'perfect' pet: a stone. A stone would not need to be fed, walked, bathed, or combed; nor would it die, become sick, or disobey. Dahl said they would be the perfect pets and joked about it with his friends. Dahl took the idea seriously. Dahl sketched an instruction manual for a pet rock. The manual was full of word games and jokes about stone like a real pet. Several times, we have heard comments like it would be as difficult as selling rocks, but this case shows us that when we think out of the box, we can get different results.

Source: https://en.wikipedia.org/wiki/Pet_Rock

I have always considered that we should surround ourselves with professionals who are smarter than we are. A few years ago, I had a teammate, a professional who had no experience in cybersecurity but had an excellent attitude. The first few weeks were intense for him because he had to learn a field new to him while finishing tasks from the previous job. However, he always had a great attitude and was willing to learn. I noticed that he spent a lot of time chatting with his peers. That never worried me because he always delivered results. It amazes me that every time I asked him for support, he would not send an email; instead, he would get up from his desk and speak directly with the person who could help us and explain what he needed. He genuinely cared about his peers. He knew their birthdays and knew how their families were doing. In just a few minutes, he would clarify any doubts and solve cases that could have taken weeks, had he chosen to send an email instead of talking face-to-face.

I gave myself the opportunity to fully learn and trust and empower my team, and we got exceptional results. Trusting and empowering my team allowed us to be more efficient, creative, and innovative. We had excellent dynamics. Once a week we had a team building meeting and assigned ourselves tasks like reading books or watching leadership films and then talking about what we had learned. Once a month, I had one-on-one meetings with each member of my team, and in that meeting, we could have a coffee and talk about the opportunities to improve things and talk about my opportunities for improvement.

I think one of the qualities of a leader is to promote new leaders. One day I was offered a job in another organization and I knew that a member of my team was the one for that position. I told him that I knew I was shooting at my foot because he was very talented, and it would be hard to fill that gap. A year before I suggested to him that he study for a master's degree in cybersecurity; a suggestion that he took seriously. That degree was a strategic differentiator that allowed him to get a new job in a brand new position, and today he is the CISO of an important multinational company.

Levitt in "Marketing Myopia" challenges us to focus not on what we sell but on what our customers' needs are. When I realized that what I do must have a purpose; but even more importantly, when I understood that my purpose is to serve, then my life changed radically, and from that moment on, everything I do can fulfill that purpose. I set out to use the phrase, "How can I serve you?" every time I receive a phone call or message; that fills me with the satisfaction that I can fulfill my purpose.

If we do a survey and ask what the brakes are for in a Ferrari, most people will respond, the brakes are used to brake (stop the car). Seeing a little further, we can understand that the purpose of the brakes is actually to allow the driver to travel faster, and the driver can indeed drive faster, because he has full confidence that when he needs to brake, the brakes will fulfill their purpose.

People are the most valuable asset that organizations have. When we give ourselves the opportunity to know other departments' goals, we can design a better strategy - a winning strategy, where everyone is part of it, and they all contribute to the success of that strategy - a winning cybersecurity culture strategy, where the organization promotes a security culture by conviction, and not because it is forced to do it. Learning is only fulfilled, when there is a change of behavior. In my experience, collaboration as a cybersecurity strategy has been the most highly effective factor in success.

"If you want to go fast, go alone. If you want to go far, go together." – African proverb

---

About the Author

Jorge Mario
President of IoT Security Institute Guatemala Chapter
Vice president of (ISC)² Guatemala Chapter
Global Security Operations Center Manager at Millicom (Tigo)
Cybersecurity Academy Director at Panamerican Business School
Awarded as the Senior Information Security Professional of America in 2017 by (ISC).²
Awarded for the Most Innovative Cybersecurity Project Globally in 2017 by the EC Council at the Global CISO Forum.

Bachelor in Telecommunications, Master in Organizational Leadership, Master in Project Management, Master in Business Administration, Master in Talent Management, Master in Cybersecurity,

Master in Data Science and Data Analysis, Master in Artificial Intelligence & Deep Learning and Ph.D. in Human Dynamics and Mental Health (thesis under review), with studies the Massachusetts Institute of Technology (MIT) in Big Data and Cybersecurity.

Holds certifications such as CISSP, C|CISO CISA, CISM, CDPSE, COBIT, ITIL, C|BP, C)PTE, C)SWAE, Lead Auditor ISO 27001, Lead Auditor ISO 22301, SCRUM, Lean Six Sigma, Design Thinking, among others.

Keynote speaker in America, Europe, and Asia.

LinkedIn Profile

Chapter 3.2

THE UNEXPECTED OPPORTUNITIES
By Morgan Craven

Always be on the lookout for unexpected opportunities

As a 19-year-old college sophomore, I wasn't expecting a phone call from an Information System Network Manager from one of the Detroit Big-3 automakers. The call was to let me know that my name came up in a lottery for an internship at the company's corporate headquarters in Auburn Hills, MI. Like a foolish kid, I turned it down on the spot because I had "big plans" for the summer. I happened to be talking to my parents later that day and was rightly scolded for not jumping on the opportunity. At the time, moving to eastern Michigan and working in the IT department for one of the big three automakers wasn't part of my plan. Later that day, I called the hiring manager and essentially told him I wasn't thinking clearly. He told me that a few other candidates had since been put ahead of me, but he'd let me know if they couldn't make it. Fortunately for me, he called back again to offer me the job. This turned out to be the first in a series of opportunities that helped me along my path to becoming an Information Security leader.

While I certainly didn't realize it at the time, the knowledge I gained in local and wide area networking in Auburn Hills opened several doors in the IT field during my last few years as an undergrad. Ultimately, all these experiences landed me a job when I graduated, working for a defense contractor on the DoD's year 2000 initiatives. Much of the IT work I did in those days was focused on consolidating different DoD systems while addressing year 2000 concerns. On one of these projects, I led a small team of integrators and developers consolidating catalog and asset management systems. During one of the first end user acceptance demos, the new application seemed very slow, clunky, and crashed multiple times. Aside from the embarrassment, my team couldn't figure out why the demo had been such dismal failure. The application had worked in our sandbox and test environments. After days of continuous troubleshooting, we came to the conclusion that something on the production network was off. At that time, the DoD agency I was working for had limited knowledge of their own network. Having no other option, I brushed off the TCP/IP skills I had developed at the automaker, got my hands on several network books, and taught myself how to use and read the outputs from a Network General Sniffer (packet capture/tracer). What I discovered was a series of network related issues, which not only caused our application to fail, but other applications that many users had been struggling with for quite some time. After sharing my findings with my own management team and the customer, they turned to my boss and asked that he task me with fixing the network. Ultimately, this led to a complete redesign of the customer network, including segmentation and introduction of the first layer-3 firewalls used by this agency. The installation of these firewalls was the beginning of my IT Security career.

Over the next 20+ years, I would lead teams of infrastructure, operations, QA, development, and security professionals. I think that many IT professionals focus on or take a seemingly logical career path towards one of these disciplines. While countless, very successful professionals have remained developers or infrastructure engineers their entire careers, I believe getting a broad experience across various IT and even business functions can help a future CISO become much more effective in his/her role as an organization's IT security leader. Effective IT security relies, in part, in understanding how systems work independently and together. Leading non-security functions provide much needed insight into operational and development frameworks. These insights make the opportunities for securing systems and processes much easier to identify and influence. Don't assume that when unexpected opportunities present themselves, that you can't grow from them. Broadening your knowledge well beyond security can be a tremendous help in a successful career.

Understand the outcomes

"Make the easy path the secure path." While I don't recall where I was the first time I heard that phrase, it's always been one that resonated with me. In general, people are like electricity in that they follow the path of least resistance. So why is this important when talking about information security and risk? Security teams have policies and controls to ensure the rules are followed, don't they? While this is hopefully true in your organization, it can be difficult to align organizational realities to the absolutes that are often associated in many InfoSec frameworks. These conflicts exist in practically all organizations regardless of size, regulated vs. non-regulated, public vs. privately owned, or government agencies.

Let's use a development team and Continuous Integration/Continuous Development (CI/CD) practice as an example. Having spent my limited development years in a now seemingly archaic waterfall software development methodology, and then supporting Agile development from an infrastructure perspective, I marvel at the speed, quality, and flexibility that CI/CD practices bring. I've also lain awake at night worrying that new risks and vulnerabilities can be created at the same rate functional capabilities are created with these modern development practices. Making things more challenging for security professionals is the end users' ability to leverage Cloud services with often little to no oversight from IT security teams. To mitigate these risks, the natural tendency for many security teams is to double down on what has worked in the past. Unfortunately, these tactics are not always effective in mitigating the risks associated with rapid development and consumption of new technologies.

In today's world, early involvement is key to influencing the outcomes you are trying to achieve. For teams leveraging CI/CD frameworks, learn their processes and identify how to plug security into these processes so that the collective team can identify issues as early as possible; for example, continually scan for vulnerabilities during the development cycles. In most cases, the development teams will prioritize fixing the issues during their standard development sprints. Identifying issues just before or after go-live will often lead to unnecessary friction between technology teams and costs, as well as missed business opportunities.

Early involvement must also extend outside of technology teams and to business teams who are evaluating or adopting technologies. Dating back to the late 1990s, when wireless or Wi-Fi technologies first came onto the scene, I worked in the logistics industry where large warehouses, truck terminals, and cross-docks were commonplace. Business teams quickly saw the value of leveraging wireless technologies within their respective operations. While very powerful, many of these Wi-Fi technologies brought with them inherent risks that weren't completely understood at the time. At that point in my career, many others in technology and I resisted the introduction and the use of these technologies because we didn't understand them. Unfortunately, we also didn't spend the necessary time to understand why the business saw so much potential value in them. I focused on the unknown risk rather than acknowledging the potential value and championing the development of a secure wireless standard that could be leveraged throughout the company business units. The result of this approach was that each business unit adopted various wireless technologies from different vendors and implemented their own version of security. In hindsight, had we spent our time advocating for the adoption of a secure wireless standard when the need for this technology was first identified, we could have made that secure path the easy path for each of our business units.

Fast forward 20 years and many security teams are trying to determine the best approach for securing Cloud technologies within their respective organizations. While each approach and rate of adoption will be different, these technologies will find their way into every organization whether sanctioned or not. Rather than putting up roadblocks, understand what's driving the business towards a technology or direction. Is the business working around IT because IT can't keep up with their needs? Are they just unaware that IT may already have the capability necessary to give them the efficiencies they are looking for? It's impossible to know unless we understand the underlying drivers to their motivations. Armed with this understanding, we can help facilitate the collaboration with all stakeholders and ultimately drive to the most secure and practical solution.

Focus on Risk

Every organization is different as they all operate in unique industries, cultures, and business models. These differences expose risks that may or may not exist from one organization to another. Every security professional has likely been part of a third-party security assessment. While these assessments can help in identifying gaps to your organization's security posture relative to established baselines, it will be up to you to understand how the identified technical or process risks relative to your organization. Understanding the relative risks to your organization is essential for focusing on the right things.

Security leaders will need to rank risks for their respective organizations, be able to justify their approach, and ultimately direct investment into security initiatives in the most effective way. Let's face it, with the constant barrage of headlines around security hacks, data loss, and inappropriate use of social media, justifying security and risk avoidance initiatives is easier than ever. Couple this with the seemingly endless supply of new security products from new or well-known vendors, it's very easy to get distracted from focusing on the most critical risks to the organization. Security leaders seemingly have lines of vendors forming outside their doors who want to pitch the latest and greatest technologies. While these technologies can be remarkable, always question the effectiveness of investing the time and money associated into new initiatives. Often, ensuring effectiveness in security fundamentals can be more valuable than layering on additional products or services. As an example, effective patching, vulnerability management, end-user training programs, modern backup strategies, and general security controls are critical to mitigating many risks. The bad guys are creative and will always find new and innovative ways to get whatever they can. It can be easy to get distracted from security fundamentals while trying to keep pace with them. Losing site of the fundamentals can often pose a greater organizational risk than an external threat.

Whether we think so or not, all security leaders will be asked to justify prior and future security investments and priorities to CIOs, CEOs, and Boards of Directors. Be prepared to discuss how the latest news headlines may impact existing risks to your organization, or potentially create unforeseen risks. Be pragmatic and don't under or overstate the risk to the organization. At the same time, realize that you will have budget constraints to live with, and additional investments will be scrutinized. I've seen IT investments made in haste as a response to an event or incident. While this is sometimes necessary, always remain cognizant that emotions will settle and you will be asked to explain decisions that may have negatively impacted the organization, as well as defend the investments made to execute those decisions. IT security is often the least understood of IT disciplines, but the most widely publicized in the media. This can make an IT security leader's job more challenging, as you not only have to contend with the internal and external organizational risk, but also must separate fact from fiction or market driven hype.

Know the "why"

Knowing why we are doing what we do seems like a basic concept, but it's especially important in driving an organizational security program. By knowing "why" we are doing something and being able to articulate the rationale, we can more effectively garner support and maintain the credibility necessary to influence the outcomes we are trying to achieve. Since security is often an area where we sometimes need to tell people "no," being able to explain the rationale behind the "no" is important. This will help foster trust with the internal and external partners we support.

Many years ago, working for a large global logistics company, I was sitting in an auditorium as part of an IT infrastructure town hall audience. On the stage were several senior IT leaders from the company. During the Q&A session, an engineer in his mid to late 20s asked a straightforward question about a well-known internal process that was the source of significant frustration among many groups. The engineer asked why this process required so much administrative overhead and took so long to complete. Nobody on stage answered the question, which led others in the audience to ask the question again. Eventually, one of the leaders onstage made the statement "that's just the way it is" in a somewhat terse tone. Based on the facial expression by the engineer who asked the original question and many others in the audience, the response from IT leadership was not well received. At that moment, a significant amount of leadership credibility was lost and much of the audience became disinterested in the remaining town hall. Rather than acknowledging the pain point, explaining at even a very high level why the process was currently the way it was or offering to follow-up with those asking the questions, the audience was told to accept it with no explanation. I don't believe the IT leader who responded the way he did ever realized how much credibility he lost that day.

By knowing why or making it a point to understand why, this can only aid in your credibility as a security leader. Without credibility, your ability to influence outcomes at a business or IT level is limited. Whether it's asking for additional budget, changing organizational or personal behaviors, or driving the adoption of policies, try to tap into the people's intellectual curiosity by explaining the "why." Explaining the "why" you are asking them to do or support is so important to the organization's success. Throughout my career, I've had individuals or groups ask about why certain policies or security controls exist. I always make it a point to answer these questions in a way that hopefully satisfies the individual or group's intellectual curiosity. In doing so, I believe I'm recruiting more people to become security champions and ultimately, deliver the organizational security outcomes I'm trying to achieve.

Aside from knowing the "why" about security, knowing your numbers is also essential. Whether the numbers are from your budget, organizational malware prevention statistics, number of legacy operating systems requiring upgrades, or a severity breakdown of key risks on your risk register, a working knowledge of these numbers can be very useful. You never know when you'll need to refer to these numbers in an elevator or hallway conversation, selling a project, or responding to stakeholders during meetings.

Secure Outcomes

Hopefully, the insights you'll gain from reading this book will help guide you in achieving your career goals. Information Security is a challenging career path but can be fascinating and rewarding at the same time. Not unlike other leadership roles, effective Information Security leaders require working knowledge of other IT disciplines as well as the organizations on behalf of which we are managing risk. Security provides for the added dimension of balancing technology risk with organizational productivity and customer demands.

Striking the right balance between risk mitigation, organizational productivity, cost, and adhering to various compliance requirements is no small task. Don't be afraid to take on opportunities that may not necessarily seem like a logical path, but broaden your knowledge of the business, your organization, or other IT functions. Know and evangelize the outcomes you are trying to achieve on behalf of your organization and understand the "why" behind the organizational or behavioral changes you are driving. If you can't effectively explain why you are asking people to change, your ability to influence will be diminished. Stay close and know your numbers. Doing so will not only aid in driving your credibility but help guide you in quantifying organizational risk and focusing on the right risk mitigation plans.

About the Author

Morgan Craven is currently the Vice President of Information Security at The Freeman Company, one of the world's leading brand experience companies. He has held various Information Technology leadership roles in the transportation, retail, financial services, and defense industries with experience managing projects, infrastructure, and product engineering teams.

LinkedIn Profile

Chapter 3.3

THE POWER OF THE ETHICS FORMULA
By Paola Saibene

The most practical guidance I can humbly recommend and provide to my fellow cybersecurity and risk management professionals, is that of cultivating and endorsing a multi-lens, holistic, ecosystem view regarding the reduction and mitigation of risk. Furthermore, I would entreat the mindful reader to solidify the convergence of the protection of digital assets, with the advocacy of the data subject, as well as the care and concern for the digitally unaware, or even the digitally marginalized - be it in varying regional, demographic, or socioeconomic conditions.

In practical terms, this means that merely honing-in the cybersecurity or the risk management skills will not be enough to deal with the complexity of the risk landscape at hand, whether in small or large organizations. Now, more than ever we are called to fuse strategy, cybersecurity, risk management, data privacy, and digital ethics in our practices and behaviors.

The evolution of technological innovation has propelled at speeds never seen before, and we, as cybersecurity and risk management practitioners, face the reality that without acute business acumen, and without looking at risk as an end-to-end value proposition to the business, we fall short of being able to remain critically relevant in the enterprise. The days of large-scale automation of compliance, risk, and cybersecurity practices are already upon us, and we must cultivate new ways of serving and leading in the new, blended world of the digital, the physical, and even the newly created, bleeding edge, trans-human or internet of bodies practices.

The recommendations below are the result of having had a long career in IT, after already having an established career as a psychologist and as a literature and linguistics professor - many thanks to my philosophy degree for helping me find rationale in varied pursuits. I used my non-technical experience to bridge humanity with the very technical and sometimes techno-centric world that I ended up calling my professional home. My observations stem from having the experience of someone who started from the bottom of the IT ladder, and worked eventually as a CIO, CTO, CSO, VP of ERM, and Global Privacy Officer of large and complex organizations.

The power of the e-t-h-i-c-s formula

At the heart of running a good cybersecurity practice, is the ability to inspire and guide others to comply and adhere to controls not for the sake of abiding by a framework or a regulation, but out of a desire to be a vital and an impactful party in the chain of organizational behaviors that can bring success by defending the users, protecting the data, and pushing back on multiple threats.

My hope is that my experience will benefit you as it pertains to expanding your horizons and leveraging the world of risk management, by having your voice be heard in a volatile, fluctuating, and ever developing digital ethics landscape, affecting the most advanced and innovative technologies and practices.

The theme of this chapter is one of centering cybersecurity within an ecosystem of risk that is overlaid by an ethical perspective, which in turn keeps the cybersecurity initiatives in context, relevant, and future-minded at the core. For this reason, I invite the reader to follow the ETHICS formula I have used over the years.

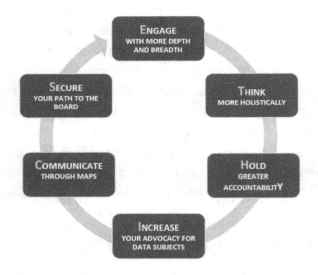

E =

• ENGAGE with MORE BREADTH and DEPTH (from the strategic board initiatives to the small marketing projects – remain engaged, alert, and aware of how all these vectors converge and greatly affect your risk and cybersecurity measures)

As a cybersecurity and risk professional we need to be well versed in what the industry in which we work considers the new ways of opening markets, how it competes in the national or global landscape, and how it shapes the culture and the behavior of the workforce. Many of these indicators reside far away from the day-to-day activities of cybersecurity, and for this reason, there is the danger that cybersecurity professionals might become isolated, less in-touch with what is going on around them, and an after-thought at the time of strategizing within the innovation team of executives. At more tactical levels, this is equally true, as software purchases, small marketing projects, and new partnerships might develop and get implemented without thorough consultation or exchange of ideas with the cyber and risk teams. It is up to the security team to insert itself in the business in a manner that they are sought after, not just for the sake of complying with policies and procedures, but for the sake of gleaning from their wisdom and expertise, so that initiatives are designed and realized with a 'security and privacy by design' mentality.

T =

- THINK MORE HOLISTICALLY – (expand your parameters by actively leveraging enterprise risk frameworks, audit frameworks, risk legal profiles, contextual data privacy findings, and ethical architectural designs)

One of the most underused and more powerful mechanisms of anchoring cybersecurity practices across the organization is to integrate them into the family of existing frameworks from other departments. From enterprise (integrated) risk management's COSO ERM and ISO 36000, for example, to product and service quality standards, such as ISO 91003, to data privacy regulations, such as GDPR and CCPA/CPRA, to ITSM service practices. The value that this brings is one of 'locking arms' with departments in a synchronous manner, by complying simultaneously with multiple controls, and bringing greater visibility to gaps and deficiencies that need more attention. It also regulates the prioritization and urgency applied to cybersecurity needs, by way of positioning them within the overall priorities of governance, risk, compliance, quality, efficiencies, and audit, as well product development and service standards.

Furthermore, a holistic mindset will lend itself to an easier application of data privacy and legal measures that will abide by the spirit of the laws in place locally or globally. This is important, because it helps to exhibit the changing value of the datasets as they traverse networks and processes across the enterprise and beyond.

H =

- HOLD GREATER ACCOUNTABILITY – (participate more intricately and have a team role in business projects leveraging technology – from the onset to the delivery – help make decisions at the design stage)

Cybersecurity teams can earn a lot of respect by participating in design thinking sessions at the project and program level, having a strong say in customer journey maps, helping write stories and epics in agile, learning to use and apply platforms of ideation, and advocating for stronger requirement management methodologies, as needed. The thorough understanding of the demands and expectations of the agile project management world, and the software development world, makes the cyber and risk professionals leapfrog ahead of the competition, as they are able to interact with a language and a modality that is entrenched in the world of innovation and software development. Knowing how to be a part of the user stories, as they are formed towards algorithmic

166

development for machine learning and artificial intelligence, will render the cyber and risk professional a seat at the table in the design phases of key projects and initiatives.

Additionally, becoming more intricately connected to machine learning and artificial intelligence experts in the organization, can help bring to light geographic, legal hurdles and data subject needs in the data privacy domain, as well as anonymization and pseudonymization requirements and nuances of delivery.

At the portfolio level, cybersecurity professionals can glean from understanding the overall investment and focus of resources, and they are better equipped to perceive what gaps exist that might affect cybersecurity and risk efforts.

I =

- INCREASE YOUR ADVOCACY FOR THE DATA SUBJECTS – (understand the potential collision of interests between protecting enterprise assets and standing up for extraterritorial, national, and local data subject rights)

Cybersecurity professionals traditionally get trained to protect data that is considered sensitive or private, yet the training required to understand an extraterritorial, contextual application of privacy laws, such as the GDPR, is often relegated to legal or compliance teams, instead. For this reason, it is crucial that security leaders step back and learn how to look at the rights of data subjects independently from the rights and privileges of the organization. Data subject rights can often collide with perceived needs of a company, and this is where legal basis for collection and retention come to play and must be reconciled. The contextual aspect of modern privacy regulations leaves the cybersecurity professional unable to find controls or frameworks that fit exactly with what is needed in some cases, and the more legal understanding they have, the better positioned they are to see how security can help mitigate or remediate issues. When contextual data privacy compliance is given to the cybersecurity team to handle, it is important to look at the information and data governance frameworks from a purely business perspective, prior to applying privacy and cybersecurity frameworks to it.

In the health industry, for instance, it is also important to have a clear picture between the difference of deontological and consequential data privacy risk, and to know which areas are regulated and which ones remain unregulated, leaving potential gaps in interpretation and understanding. It is here, where it is helpful to see the resolutions through the eyes of the data subject as well as the organization, simultaneously.

C =

- COMMUNICATE THROUGH MAPS (overcome urgency and prioritization challenges by mapping dependencies in business terms, with clear KPI, KRI, and KGI rankings)

The world of communicating risk and issues, and subsequently acting upon them, is riddled with friction and contentions that tend to stem from opposing priorities and needs amongst departments. For this reason, I have found it particularly helpful to convey risk and its dependencies through well-crafted mapping systems that take away the focus on the people and the departments, and places it on inputs, processes, and outputs/outcomes instead. This avoids much of the blame-game that you often see in risk and security meetings with stakeholders, and instead it elevates the dialogue to educate all parties on how interconnected the danger zones are, and it invites them to be part of the solution by ranking and prioritizing the mitigation and remediation steps collaboratively. Moreover, it is through these mapping exercises, that colleagues can agree on and calibrate the impact that cybersecurity and risk gaps can have in key performance indicators and key governance indicators, and they can walk away with a plan of action that lets them see key risk indicators as it pertains to their particular departments.

S =

- SECURE YOUR PATH TO THE BOARD (learn to articulate security and risk issues in actionable board and executive language, understanding their pressures and concerns from a competitive market viewpoint)

It is likely that the board of directors of the company or organization that you work for is facing increasing pressure from local and global issues that take over the bulk of their attention. This often leaves little room for fruitful cybersecurity or data privacy dialogues that are generally viewed as more of an exercise in compliance, rather than a solid opportunity to bring a competitive advantage to the organization. This means that the more you learn about those other board pressures and demands, the more you can help connect them to the world of cybersecurity and risk management and thereby bring forth solutions that are not conceived in isolation, but that are presented as an intricately woven and helpful path forward that can address multiple issues at once. In essence, what you provide in these exchanges has a greater business value, and it will be accepted more eagerly by those that would have otherwise found it as a mere operational cost factor. Learning about what the professional board organizations instruct members on how to look at cyber and risk issues, will help the reader articulate and present requests, concerns, and needs in a way that fits the language and perspective of the board members. By way of becoming familiar with their quarterly magazines, monthly podcasts, etc. the cybersecurity and risk professional can meet the audience exactly where they are at and convey a more powerful and focused message.

Last thoughts...

My hope is that upon the conclusion of this chapter, the reader will be able to form an actionable plan of further engagement for themselves, their peers, and their work communities; whereby they would equip themselves with the ability to contribute more meaningfully and more impactfully within the realm of cybersecurity, risk management, governance, compliance, privacy, audit, and digital ethics.

May such contributions be elevated to the strategic and innovation decisions and dialogues held by the Board of Directors, and by the team of executives charged with leading the organization.

This profession can often feel overwhelming. With so much ground to cover and not enough capacity or resources to do so, it is easy to lose heart and think that our contribution is not impactful enough. However, we must remember that, although potentially far removed from a chain of catastrophic events, our efforts may be the only ones standing between a criminal entity and victims that would be unable to recover from the crime.

Approximately 20 years ago, I met someone who was helping an elderly lady who had lost all her retirement, her home, and any cash left in her bank account, as a result of breaches that had taken place over a period of three months. She had trusted an individual who executed a sophisticated digital scam, leaving her penniless within the year. The authorities found that none of the assets and lifesavings of this woman amounted to a figure that merited further investigation, being themselves overwhelmed by these requests and having to put a dollar baseline to the types of cybercrime that their time and resources would allow them to pursue. In other words, she was left alone, with nothing, and with no help at hand.

The latter part of this story was more heartbreaking to me than the former. What is someone like this elderly lady to do? The question I decided to pose to myself was, how can I have an impact that would minimize such cases, by way of building strong and active communities of protection that would be entrenched in the decisions, strategy, design, implementation, configuration, and execution of technology initiatives and that would have, at their very core, cybersecurity, risk mitigation, and data privacy in mind, and would uphold the highest possible standards, while still delivering in a timely manner that would ensure keeping up with the competition.

I invite you to be part of such a community. May we stand in the gap for those who can't and may we find contentment in always doing the right thing – for everyone.

About the Author

Paola Saibene has spent 25 years in IT. She is a former Chief Information Officer, Chief Technology Officer, Chief Strategy Officer, VP of Enterprise Risk Management, and Global Privacy Officer. She has spent her career working in large, multi-billion-dollar organizations with global scope, and she has received multiple awards for IT innovation and digital transformation. She has also received a Governor's commendation for her cybersecurity initiatives. Paola has led many large-scale technology rollouts, while designing approaches that sustain cybersecurity, contextual data privacy, compliance, and overall risk management at the core of the initiatives.

Presently, Paola is the CEO at Quartus Factor, a company focused on increasing resiliency and strength in organizations. She is an adjunct faculty member at Georgetown University, (ENAE) Panamerican Business School, and Dallas Baptist University, where she is also the founder and Chair of the Center of Excellence in Digital Ethics.

She holds an M.S.C.P. in Psychology, M.A. in Literature and Linguistics, and a bachelor's degree in philosophy, having practiced as a psychologist, and having taught literature and linguistics, prior to her career as a technologist.

LinkedIn Profile

www.ingramcontent.com/pod-product-compliance
Lightning Source LLC
La Vergne TN
LVHW051235050326
832903LV00028B/2424